PRAISE FOR DR. DON GREENE

"Musicians face an intensely competitive orchestral job market and the reality that a three-minute audition can determine a lifelong career. Don Greene's *Audition Success* gives young musicians a concrete set of skills to achieve the concentrated focus needed in these critical moments."

—Michael Tilson Thomas,
Music Director, San Francisco Symphony and
Artistic Director, New World Symphony

"Before working with Dr. Greene, I was too preoccupied with the 'what-ifs' while I was playing. However, through his methods of centering and visualization, among others, my concentration and sense of focus has since drastically improved my performance on many levels. This book is a 'must-have' for anyone who wants to beat their own mind games!"

—Julia Pilant, Principal Horn, Syracuse Symphony

"This book should have a very positive impact on the performing arts profession. In particular, it gives an exceptional focus to prepare musicians for the rigors that they will encounter in their careers."

—Joseph Polisi, President, The Juilliard School

"Dr. Greene's ability to enhance performing skills is amazing. He is a tremendous asset to both professional and aspiring artists."

—Joe Illick, Lake George Opera

"Dr. Greene helped me to become confident, free, and courageous with my singing. I use his centering technique when I audition—now I focus completely on my singing, and not on what others may be thinking of me. Since working with Dr. Greene, I perform better and have won auditions consistently."

—Penny Shumate, opera singer

Performance Success

ALSO BY DON GREENE, Ph.D.

Fight Your Fear and Win
Audition Success

Performance Success

PERFORMING YOUR BEST UNDER PRESSURE

Don Greene, Ph.D.

Routledge
A THEATRE ARTS BOOK
New York and London

Published in 2002 by
Routledge
29 West 35th Street
New York, NY 10001

Published in Great Britain by
Routledge
11 New Fetter Lane
London EC4P 4EE

Routledge is an imprint of the Taylor & Francis Group.

Printed in the United States of America on acid-free paper.

10 9 8 7 6 5 4

Library of Congress Cataloging-in-Publication Data
Greene, Don.
    Performance Success : performing your best under pressure / Don Greene.
    p. cm.
  Includes bibliographical references.
  ISBN 0-87830-122-4 (acid-free paper)
    1. Music—Performance—Psychological aspects. 2. Performance anxiety. 3. Success—Psychological aspects. 4. Self-help techniques. I. Title.

ML3830.G74 2001
781.4'3—dc21
                                         2001031912

*This book is dedicated to my musical mentors
Ed Castillano, Joe Illick, and Julie Landsman.*

*Thank you for sharing your profound wisdom,
professional example, and love ever since
you welcomed me into your special world.*

Acknowledgments

The material in this book comes from three main sources: my graduate course at The Juilliard School in New York, a series of master classes at the New World Symphony in Miami Beach, and workshops conducted at the OperaWorks Intensive Program in Los Angeles.

Let me first express my appreciation to the faculty and staff at Juilliard: Joseph Polisi, Stephen Clapp, Karen Wagner, David Wakefield, Dorothy DeLay, Lauren Schiff, Elaine Douvas, Carol Wincenc, Sharon Isbin, Jane Gottlieb, Stephen Pier, Al Miner, Ray Mase, Joe Alessi, Laurie Carter, Tom Nazelli, Janet Kisson, Jane Rubinsky, Carol Adrian, Andy King, Warren Deck, Daniel Cataneo, Virginia Allen, Toby Appel, Jerome Ashby, Julius Baker, Jeanne Baxtresser, Itzhak Perlman, and Pamela Pyle. Thank you for giving a sports psychologist a chance with your precious students. I'm honored to be able to call you colleagues.

I am very grateful to Michael Tilson Thomas, Pat Nott, Fergus Scarfe, Michael Linville, Chris Dunworth, Ron Stone, Doug Merilatt, and Candice Flores of the New World Symphony. You have created such an ideal environment for musicians to develop and grow. It is delightful working with you and the Fellows and watching them flourish.

The OperaWorks Intensive Program in Los Angeles provides a marvelous and fun proving grounds for artists. My deepest thanks go to Ann Baltz, David Aks, and Julia Aks, the fantastic staff of Dee Noah, Mark Lawson, John Ballerino, Eli Villanueva, Phillip Young, Michael Ellison, Carolynne Dale Levine, Martha Gerhart, and Gregory Buchalter, and the singers who were ready to run with this information.

My sincerest gratitude goes to Laura Greenwald for her kind and gracious help throughout this project. Many thanks go to Kevin Hanek, for his artistry and guidance, and Gwendolyn Freed for her editorial expertise and musical insight. Working on this project with you was a great joy. I am also grateful to Bill Germano, T. J. Mancini, Henry Bashwiner, and Matt Byrnie from Routledge for getting this to print.

Finally let me say thanks to Margie Danilow, Gina Browning, Elma Linz Kanefield, Bob Fox, Jerry Zampino, Jerry Hunton, Michelle Baker, Tony Cecere, Richard Chandler, Colleen Gaetano, Camille Gifford, David Geber, Polly Bergen, Sharon Daniels, Dan Sullivan, Claire Johnson, Tom and Karen Kamp, Paul Navarro, Peter Stewart, Floyd Cooley, Gail Williams, Keith Dobbs, and Michelle Wrighte. I thank God for your friendship and love.

Contents

Foreword

This year I had the pleasure of seeing one of my most gifted students, Jennifer Montone, win the associate principal horn audition with the Dallas Symphony. While still my student at Juilliard, she won the third horn position with the New Jersey Symphony. Talent alone could explain her success. But I know—every musician knows—that it takes something more than talent to win auditions and perform consistently at the very peak of one's powers.

It takes what Don Greene has to offer.

I first heard of Don's work in the fall of 1995 when I read an article about him in the ICSOM* newsletter. The article focused on how he had helped a horn player who'd blown countless auditions win a position with the Houston Symphony. My eyes lit up; I knew I could use that mental edge. You need everything on your side as a professional musician—even if you've been principal horn with the Metropolitan Opera for 17 years. Here was a method, a scientific approach I could put into practice. Here was a program I could share with my students.

I called Don, who was then living in California, and I said, "Where are you? I need you. My students need you. *New York* needs you."

For the next six months or so I became his client and after he moved to Manhattan, his musical mentor as well. He worked on getting my overactive left brain critic under control, and I worked on getting him on the faculty at Juilliard, where I had him coach my students in a series of master classes. It was a new focus for both of us.

---

*International Conference of Symphony and Opera Musicians

I knew that I had lost something in my years at the Met, something I wanted back: joy. Performing night after night had started to feel like hard work. The pressure of having to be at my absolute best for every performance had cut me off from my heart. The perfectionist in me was getting in the way of the artist.

I already had some coping skills. Years of yoga had helped me discover the power of the mind. I learned that if in a deeply relaxed state, I pictured myself performing confidently, in fact that was how I actually performed. I had also trained for years in the Carmine Caruso method, which teaches your body to respond reflexively in a performance rather than reflectively—much as athletes learn to trust their muscle memory. I had some appreciation for the importance of using the creative right brain over the left when it came to performing under pressure.

But Don's method was so tangible, so organized. You took a test; you got a diagnosis; and he mapped out a path to a cure. Within a matter of weeks, I was playing more and more in my right brain and seeing pictures—colors!—for sounds. I could literally see what I wanted to hear. The imagery helped me form a ritual, a ritual that would ensure that I stayed reflexive and creative before and during a performance. Gradually, I found myself reveling in an almost fiery light when I played. I could now choose to not judge or analyze, and instead play from my right brain. I had access to my heart. My spirit.

The effect has been cumulative. I feel I've moved up the slippery slope all musicians grapple with, away from that place where I was struggling to a plateau of comfort, freedom, and yes, joy. I've seen my students under Don's tutelage make that same progress and that, too, fills me with joy. Now, with *Performance Success,* many more musicians will likewise get the leg up, the boost in their careers that talent alone cannot confer. Don's program is the missing ingredient, the science I so wish had been part of my early training, the methodology which can transform auditions into opportunity and performances into exultation.

What you hold in your hands is Don Greene, performance coach, in a book. What you're about to enjoy—if you get your butt in gear and do the work—is performance success.

Julie Landsman
Metropolitan Opera Orchestra
July, 2001

Performance Success

Introduction

T HE PRESSURES OF PERFORMING music are so intense, so daunting, that few in the business dare so much as broach the topic. It's taboo. As a musician you face a lifetime of auditions, competitions, recitals, solos, premieres, and debut appearances. Yours is a profession in which the slightest slip of the finger or quiver of the vocal chords can sour all the promise in the world. Yet utter the word *anxiety* backstage at a performance, and watch people's reactions. It's like you have kooties.

Divulge your inner fears in a private lesson, and the response may not be much more helpful. Many teachers prefer to stick to what they know best, which is music, not psychology. They want to help, but don't know how. So most sidestep students' apprehension. "Just relax" is the conventionally proffered advice.

Relax at the Tchaikovsky competition? Relax when you've blown $900 to fly across the country for your two-minute audition for the only symphony flute job to come open this year? Relax when your symphony job security depends on near-perfect technique in each and every concert until you're tenured? I don't think so.

I'm here to tell you that you shouldn't try to relax. It doesn't work. Physical relaxation may be the key to all kinds of mechanical functions in music, from bow hold to posture to air pressure. But relaxation in the conventional sense—as in lying on a beach in Hawaii—is a coping strategy doomed to failure. If you're relaxed right before an important performance, something's wrong. Maybe the event doesn't mean that much to you, in which case I'd advise you to consider another vocation. Or maybe you've taken too many beta blockers. In any case, if you want to be relaxed, stay at home and perform in your living room.

You can deny the problems of stress in performance or you can face them, even learn to embrace them. You can work on performing well under pressure—not just how to beat nerves but how to make them work for you. That's where I come in.

My fascination with the psychology of performance goes back to my childhood days on Long Island. I started out in gymnastics when I was seven. At ten, when I switched to diving and began to compete, I became intrigued with the question of why I could dive well in some competitions and not in others, why in some events, no matter how well I prepared, I just got nervous and sometimes missed even my easiest dives. Like a musician on the concert stage who just screwed up a simple passage, I'd be downcast, shaking my head and wondering why.

In my senior year of high school, I received an athletic appointment to the U.S. Military Academy at West Point. There I learned how to win serious competitions under adverse conditions. Afterward, I went through paratrooper and commando training, and was the first in my West Point class to be selected for the army's Special Forces, known as the Green Berets. I served on the staff at the headquarters of the John F. Kennedy Center for Unconventional Warfare.

My military experience presented me with many challenges and taught me valuable lessons. Later I would find numerous applications for these outside the military arena. They have helped my musician clients; they can help you, too.

After I got out of the army, I wanted to learn more about athletes' performance under stress, so I went back to school and attained a doctorate in psychology. My dissertation tested the use of *Centering*, a focusing strategy proven effective with competitive athletes. I wanted to see if it could help members of the San Diego Police SWAT team perform better under extremely high stress.

The SWAT team was randomly divided into two groups. One received no special training. The other got instruction and practice in Centering. Then both groups went through a high-stress shooting course. It was a "move and shoot" drill involving live ammunition. One at a time, the officers would run into a building where a series of surprise targets would pop up in pairs. One of the targets might be a guy with a machine gun and the other target would be a woman holding a baby or a bag of groceries. Despite the stress, they were supposed to shoot the guy with the machine gun and not the woman.

The officers who used Centering before they went into the building made significantly better judgments in their target selection. They shot more hostile targets and fewer innocents than did the control group. Under the extreme stress, they made better split-second decisions. Centering helped the trained officers perform better under pressure, just as it helped athletes.

After I graduated, I worked with the U.S. Olympic diving team, the World Championship swimming team and *Golf Digest* schools. A few years later I was hired by the Vail Ski School to teach its instructors how to use sports psychology with students. In the summer I conducted golf clinics. Then came a chance encounter that would lead me in a new direction altogether.

I got a call from Ed Castilano, principal bassist with the Syracuse Symphony. He was in Vail at the time, playing in a music festival and enjoying a little golf, one of his favorite hobbies. Ed was having trouble with his putting. He'd heard about my work and sought me out in hopes of improving his game.

We met at the golf course. I gave him a sports psychology survey that I developed to measure how well athletes focus under pressure, how anxiety affects their performance, and what mental skills they need to improve on. Once scored, the survey revealed Ed's strengths and weaknesses. I knew immediately what we needed to do. At the conclusion of our two days together, Ed's putting had improved dramatically.

But that wasn't the only thing. Ed said that every lesson he learned from me on the golf course had direct application to his work as a symphony player. He asked if I would be interested in working with musicians. I said that I would love it, if he would help me translate the athlete's survey into musicians' language.

I went to the Syracuse Symphony several months later with the Artist's Performance Survey in hand. At the beginning of one of the rehearsals, I stood on the conductor's podium and introduced myself. I said that I was a sports psychologist and was not sure if I had anything of value to offer them. But I was willing to try. On the first day, thirty people came to my lecture. They were mostly section players from the orchestra.

Word spread, and on the next day, sixty people attended. On the final day, almost everyone turned up, including the concert-master and most of the principal-chair players.

I was backstage at one of the Syracuse concerts when I was approached by a principal player (since retired). He was about to go onstage for a piece with an exposed solo entrance, and he was very worried about it. Nervous tension had been a problem for him since he began his performing career decades before. He'd tried hypnosis, biofeedback, relaxation training, beta blockers—everything, it seemed. He said that he was still a mess and that everybody in the orchestra knew he struggled, especially with pieces like the one he was about to be called upon to execute. He didn't care about the audience as much as he did about the respect of his fellow musicians.

I could see that he was shaking. He had to go out in fifteen minutes, and he really didn't know whether he could do it or not. He hadn't slept well lately; his blood pressure was up. I fully appreciated at this moment the incredible stress that musicians must deal with on a regular basis. And yet this man had few skills with which to effectively address these challenges. His distress touched me, and motivated me to do what I could.

Later that year, with help from the concert pianist, conductor, and opera coach Joe Illick, I refined my Artist's Performance Survey. I made a return trip to the Syracuse Symphony the next year; in group lectures and individual sessions I explained the survey, what the individual scores meant, and specifically what each player could do to improve his or her performance.

On the last day I was there, one of the orchestra's horn players told me that he had an audition coming up in two months for the Houston Symphony. He really wanted the job and asked if I could help. I said that we might be able to do it. If we could spend one hour a week for the next eight weeks on the phone, I would try my best to prepare him for the audition. He gave me his permission to tape our conversations.

That summer, I gave some master classes at the Lake George Opera Festival, where I met a young mezzo-soprano. She had an audition looming in eight weeks for the Chicago Lyric Opera. She wanted the job with all her heart, but she had trouble winning auditions. Since we had already gone over her survey, I offered to work with her by phone, just as I had with the horn player. She, too, gave me permission to tape calls.

After she and the horn player won their respective auditions, I had the tapes transcribed and put into my book *Audition Success*.

Around this time a mention of me in the newsletter *Senza Sordino* caught the attention of Julie Landsman, a faculty member at The Juilliard School and principal French horn with the Metropolitan Opera Orchestra. She asked me to work with four of her students who were preparing for a Met Orchestra audition. I spent a few months with them. Of the fifty-nine candidates at the audition, those who worked with Julie and me came in first, second, fourth, and fifth.

I moved to New York and began working full-time with performing artists. I taught in master classes with Julie Landsman at Juilliard and was later invited to work with the New World Symphony in Miami Beach. I have been very fortunate since then; many of my artists have won professional auditions, even as the competition gets tougher for fewer positions. I am now on the faculty at Juilliard, and I work extensively with musicians at major orchestras and music schools around the country.

As my clients know, and you'll soon see for yourself, the *Performance Success* process takes work. To begin, you'll take the Artist's Performance Survey and score it. That's the first step; as you move through the book you'll find out what each of your scores mean. You'll digest substantial material on how we as humans tend to respond to high-pressure conditions. You'll complete a number of challenging exercises tailored to your specific needs. And you'll go on to apply your new skills under increasing pressure and adversity. The more you use these tools, the better you'll perform. Just follow along.

And know that you are not alone.

One of the biggest fears of my life at one time was public speaking. I always got really nervous. My throat dried up, and got very tight, and I usually choked. It was painful. I will never forget a presentation I had to give during my senior year at West Point. It was not meant to be a major thing—just a five-minute talk to a small group of my classmates. Despite the fact that I had prepared extensively, I could not sleep at all the night before. When the time came, my face got red, and I stuttered and shook. A few seconds after I started, my mind went completely blank.

Years later, I went to my first and last Toast Masters meeting. As you probably know, Toast Masters is a national association that conducts group meetings to help people overcome the fear of public speaking. All you have to do is show up with a brown-bag lunch and join other nervous people around a conference table. It's supposed to be nonthreatening. First-timers are asked simply to introduce themselves and say where they live. It really isn't that big a deal, since everyone is usually from the same city. All I had to do was say, "Hi, I'm Don from San Diego."

I sat stiff and full of dread as I watched the introductions go around the table. One by one, people said their names and that they were from San Diego. When they got to about three people from me, I got up and left! I was scared. It was torture.

Years passed before I worked through this problem. Now I actually enjoy giving presentations. I've even received awards for my public-speaking ability. But I still remember what the fear felt like and what it did to me. It was devastating. So take it from me: if I could learn how to get past that, any trained performer certainly can.

From this point on, the process is much like a music lesson. When you meet a new teacher, you explain what you feel you do well and what you don't, and what you have done to address various problems. Eventually you start to play. The teacher then diagnoses your problems, offers solutions, and assigns exercises specific to your needs. When the lesson's over you go home and apply the solutions in practice. The *Performance Success* process works the same way. In the weeks to come you will find yourself toting this book around like a volume of études.

Your first step is to take the Artist's Performance Survey and score it. I encourage those with access to the World Wide Web to complete it at my Web site (DONGREENE.com). Now, at the stroke of a key, you'll get your scores immediately. Whether you do it on the Web or the old-fashioned way—by hand in the Appendix of this book—find a good time to do it, when you're not distracted by anything. This is your opportunity in effect to snap a vivid "before" picture of your current performance tendencies. So make it count.

Finally, be advised, this book is not intended to be light bedtime reading. It's going to call upon you to face some tough challenges and take courageous and meaningful action. Make real space and quality time for this work. It will pay off for you, I promise.

All the best!

Don Greene, Ph.D.
August, 2001

1. Artist's Performance Survey

Take Stock of Your Strengths and Weaknesses

P LEASE SET ASIDE at least fifteen minutes to respond to the following questions. Keep in mind that objectivity is critical. Make sure that your answers reflect how you genuinely think, feel, and behave when rehearsing and performing—not as you think you should or wish you would.

Respond with:

5 = very true for you
4 = somewhat true
3 = unsure or sometimes
2 = not very true
1 = untrue for you

SCENARIO 1

Imagine yourself on the way to rehearse or perform.

1. I have a strong inner drive to be my best.
2. The level at which I perform is very important to me.
3. I have a strong will to succeed.
4. I am driven from within.
5. I know how to perform under pressure.
6. I am commited to be the best I can be.
7. I have no fear of success.

1. _____
2. _____
3. _____
4. _____
5. _____
6. _____
7. _____

8. Going into most perfomance situations, I expect to do well.   8. _____

9. I have what it takes to make it.   9. _____

10. I perform well when I'm feeling energized and "up."   10. _____

11. I'm not afraid of failing.   11. _____

12. I believe in my talent and abilities.   12. _____

13. I have fought my way out of many difficult circumstances.   13. _____

14. I have an intense focus.   14. _____

15. I direct my full attention to what I'm doing in the moment.   15. _____

16. I am able to keep focused for as long as necessary.   16. _____

17. I'm not distracted by people moving around me or making noise.   17. _____

18. I don't worry about what other people think of my performing.   18. _____

19. I get anxious before some practice sessions.   19. _____

20. Final rehearsals can make me feel very uptight.   20. _____

21. I can get nervous just thinking about an upcoming dress rehearsal.   21. _____

22. Before important performances, I feel extremely nervous.   22. _____

23. I have no trouble getting my energy up for performances.   23. _____

24. Auditions can place overwhelming stress on me.   24. _____

25. I usually go into auditions with way too much anxiety.   25. _____

Scenario 2

Now see yourself warming up and getting ready to begin.

26. I worry about performing below my capabilities.   26. _____

27. I want to gain others' recognition of my talent.

27. _____

28. I tend to doubt my ability before I even begin.

28. _____

29. My approach to most performances is one of caution.

29. _____

30. Things never seem to work out the way I want them to.

30. _____

31. No matter how well I prepare, something just seems to go wrong.

31. _____

32. I don't do very well when I'm at a high energy level.

32. _____

33. I perform much better when I'm feeling relatively calm.

33. _____

34. It's often difficult for me to get relaxed enough.

34. _____

35. I don't know how to control my nervousness.

35. _____

36. Even the thought of doing my absolute best can make me anxious.

36. _____

37. I get too caught up in what others think of me and my performance.

37. _____

38. I have a strong fear of failure.

38. _____

39. My performance skills suffer suffer significantly under pressure.

39. _____

40. I'd probably start off better if I believed more in myself.

40. _____

41. I would not describe my focus as being powerful.

41. _____

42. I get distracted when other performers make mistakes.

42. _____

43. The main source of distraction is my own mind.

43. _____

44. I have trouble staying focused.

44. _____

45. My mind races with instructions, criticism, or totally unrelated thoughts.

45. _____

46. I say things to myself while performing that I'd never say to a friend.

46. _____

47. I'd probably do better if I didn't try so hard.

47. _____

48. It takes me a while to get it back after making mistakes.

48._____

49. I get really negative and self-critical.

49._____

50. I need to stop trying to force things to happen.

50._____

Scenario 3

Now you are performing and experiencing some problems.

51. Things do not usually go how I'd like them to go.

51._____

52. I seem to get more than my share of bad breaks.

52._____

53. I don't do very well when I'm feeling a lot of pressure.

53._____

54. I usually do better when I'm feeling relaxed.

54._____

55. I feel relatively calm in most rehearsals.

55._____

56. I worry constantly about making mistakes in performances.

56._____

57. I wish I could to do a better job of controlling my nerves.

57._____

58. I tend to start out tentatively.

58._____

59. It takes me too long to calm myself down.

59._____

60. I get distracted when a number of things all happen at once.

60._____

61. I tend to try too hard under pressure.

61._____

62. I don't focus very well.

62._____

63. Sometimes success isn't worth the effort it requires.

63._____

64. I'd probably do better if I were more self-motivated.

64._____

65. I don't always have to do my absolute best.

65._____

66. It takes me some time to recover after making a mistake.

66._____

67. I really get down on myself.

67._____

68. It's difficult getting my energy up after something bad has happened.

68._____

69. Sometimes my energy is not up enough in certain performances.

69._____

70. My energy has even been too low in some auditions.

70._____

71. I have trouble keeping my mind in the present.

71._____

72. I have a short attention span.

72._____

73. I go back to my mistakes or ahead to things that could go wrong.

73._____

74. I even worry about the possibility of performing too well.

74._____

75. I need to focus better.

75._____

SCENARIO 4

After resolving some of the problems, you are about to finish.

76. I believe that things usually turn out for the best.

76._____

77. I have the ability to bounce back after unfortunate circumstances.

77._____

78. It does not take me very long to get back on track.

78._____

79. Tough conditions bring out the fighter in me.

79._____

80. Even if I'm tired, I can summon up my energy and rally.

80._____

81. I know how to get myself "pumped up" when I need to.

81._____

82. I like to go onstage feeling up.

82._____

83. I enjoy performing with a lot of positive energy.

83._____

84. I am willing to take certain risks to see how good I can be.

84._____

85. I am not afraid of the consequences of doing my very best.

85._____

86. I'm not that concerned with what others may think.

86._____

87. Auditions don't make me all that nervous.

87._____

88. I know that I will be successful.   88. ____

89. I am very driven for my own reasons.   89. ____

90. I am commited to doing my best.   90. ____

91. I would do almost anything to succeed.   91. ____

92. I know how to function under pressure.   92. ____

93. I can focus even in distracting surroundings.   93. ____

94. I talk to myself in a positive way.   94. ____

95. I center myself in the "here and now."   95. ____

96. I am able to still the chatter in my mind before I begin.   96. ____

97. I quietly focus on the task at hand.   97. ____

98. I summon up the courage and "Go For It" *no matter what.*   98. ____

99. I am able to trust my talent and abilities and "Let It Go."   99. ____

100. I keep focused until I am done.   100. ____

Congratulations on completing your survey. You can have it scored at my Web site (DONGREENE.com) or follow the scoring instructions in the Appendix.

2. Your Musical Benchmark
Make a "Before" Tape

I T'S TIME FOR YOU to make an audio or video tape, to establish a benchmark of your current level of performance abilities. It will serve as the "before" picture that will demonstrate your progress over the coming weeks. The live recording process is intended to simulate the conditions of moderate performance pressure. So please adhere closely to the instructions below.

Choose three contrasting excerpts or solos. Start with a relatively easy selection, move on to a mid-level one, and finish with something very challenging. The total length of the works performed back to back should be from fifteen to thirty minutes.

Set everything up ahead of time. Make sure that your performance space is ready and that your equipment is in order. Feel free to invite some colleagues, acquaintances, or family members to the recording session.

Take as long as you would like before beginning to perform, but once the tape is rolling, keep going. Do not stop until you reach the end, no matter what happens. You may pause briefly—less than twenty seconds—between selections.

Immediately after you've finished, make a few comments on the tape about how you performed. Please give each piece a subjective rating on a scale from 1 to 100, with 1 being your worst nightmare and 100 being great. Cite examples of what you did well and what could have been better.

If you have listeners present, ask them to speak into the tape recorder, rating and commenting on your performance. If you do not have listeners present at the session, give someone the tape soon afterward. Write down the score he or she gives you as well as his or her comments. Don't forget to label the tape with your name, the date, and the word *Before*.

Taping #1

DATE: _____ TIME: _____ LOCATION: _____

Part/Piece Excerpt	*Rating*	*Strengths*	*Areas to Improve*
_____	_____	_____	_____
_____	_____	_____	_____
_____	_____	_____	_____

EVALUATOR'S NAME: _____ DATE: _____

Part/Piece Excerpt	*Rating*	*Comments*
_____	_____	_____
_____	_____	_____
_____	_____	_____

---

3. Under the Hot Lights

Learn How Stress Affects You

I FEEL NOTHING BUT AWE and appreciation for elite-level musicianship, but my work in the field has proved one thing, if nothing else. When the proverbial chips are down, it doesn't matter how fast you can trill, what conservatory you attended, or what chorus you sing in: stress can make you or break you.

Every artist is unique, but when the pressure's on, all performances fall neatly into three distinct categories. They are *Suboptimal Performance, Optimal Performance,* and *Peak Performance.* You'll be thinking a lot about them in this book.

In Suboptimal Performance, you're falling far short of your genuine capabilities. In Optimal Performance, you're performing quite well, though not necessarily at the absolute height of your potential. It's important to know that many successful performers do most of their performing at the Optimal level. This, very often, is just fine.

In Peak Performance, you've attained the ever-elusive ideal: everything seems magically to come together and the music virtually performs itself. Wonderful, even magnificent, things happen in Peak Performance. We'd all love to spend as much time as possible in this elevated state. But you can't get there without first understanding what Optimal Performance is all about. Optimal Performance is the focus of this workbook.

Let's first look at the potential negative effects that stress can have on performers. Much of the pioneering work in this area was done by Robert Nideffer, Ph.D., a world-renowned sports psychologist. Dr. Nideffer developed *The Stress Model* to explain what can happen to performers—even elite ones—under pressure.

Stress is any real or imagined fear, threat, danger, sudden surprise, or shock—anything that puts extra pressure on you. Every day and most nights of your life, you as a performer must face stress in the form of such events as lessons, recitals, juries, auditions, and solos. And as often as not, the work you do in the practice room entails some degree of stress as well.

> *Stress can make you or break you.*

What you feel under stress may be unwelcome, but it's normal, all of it. Stress is a human condition, integral to the structure and functioning of our bodies and minds. Its negative effects tend to manifest in two ways: physical and mental.

THE STRESS MODEL

SITUATIONAL STRESSORS

Real or imagined dangers
Competitive environments
Ambiguous/Unknown situations

PHYSICAL RESPONSE

- Increased heart rate
- Changes in respiration
- Muscle tension
- Feeling unsteady
- Increased perspiration

PSYCHOLOGICAL RESPONSE

- Feeling confused
- Loss of focus
- Mental rigidity
- Inner-directed attention
- Tunnel vision

PERFORMANCE CONSEQUENCES

- Physical: impairment of timing and fine motor coordination; jerky movements
- Mental: faulty decision making caused by inflexible, indecisive, or impulsive thinking
- Focus: distracted by inner noise, unable to concentrate on the task at hand

The physical effects of stress are myriad. Your pulse increases. Your heart may feel like it's pounding out of your chest. Your breathing gets faster, higher up in your lungs, and shallower; some people actually hyperventilate under stress. Increased stomach acid produces the feeling known as "butterflies." (The feeling really *is* in your stomach, not your head.) These and other symptoms combine to create what's known as the *fight-or-flight syndrome*. It goes back to Neanderthal days, when cavemen encountered saber-toothed tigers about as often as we encounter Starbucks today. Facing the beasts, cavemen had two choices: they could run away or they could use their increased energy to fight.

> *What you feel under stress may be unwelcome, but it's normal—all of it.*

Our bodies and certain primitive parts of our brains really haven't changed much since then. The tigers may be gone, but for performers especially, stressors abound. And they set in motion the same hardwired responses. Your stepped-up heart rate sends more energy to your large muscles and extremities. Your hands start to shake, you start to perspire, you get clammy palms or you need to make repeated trips to the bathroom. Your body is gearing up, preparing to respond to stress because, unfortunately, it doesn't know the difference between a tiger and the solo horn part to Richard Strauss's *Till Eulenspiegels lustige Streiche*.

True stories prove that a mother, seeing her child pinned under a car, can lift a vehicle off the ground. If you've ever tried with a group of friends to pick up a car, even a Volkswagen Beetle, you know that it's not easy. What summons superhuman strength in a crisis is *adrenaline*. Once released into the bloodstream, this powerful hormone primes the human body very effectively to fight or flee.

> *As adrenaline flows into your bloodstream, you have no outlet.*

Unfortunately, as a performing artist, you can do neither. As adrenaline floods your bloodstream, you have no outlet. With the famous flute solo from Brahms' Fourth Symphony coming up in a few bars, there's nothing you can do but sit still—not much of a physical workout. Meanwhile, your frustrated fight-or-flight response makes its merry way to your extremities, bringing on sweat, hand tremors, feelings of unsteadiness, and a whole constellation of other major and minor symptoms.

Of these, muscle tension poses the greatest threat to your performance. As much as you may loathe them, most other stress symptoms have a relatively minor impact on your capacity to perform. Muscle tension is the big one. In music and sports alike, tight muscles result in poor performance.

Most people automatically brace and tighten up under stress. It's that primitive response. You're driving way too fast as you take an off-ramp and head into a tight turn. As you hit the brakes, what do your hands and shoulders do? They instinctively tense up. But for performers, that response can be devastating. So be as nervous or energized as you want, but learn how to stay physically relaxed. Good performances are almost always the result of relatively relaxed muscles. We'll focus on this in depth later in the book. For right now, simply pay attention to the difference between your physical tension level when you're practicing at home versus what you feel like in a recital, audition, dress rehearsal, or opening night.

> *Muscle tension poses the greatest threat to your performance.*

We tend to tighten up in the very muscles we need to keep most relaxed. Singers and wind players tend to tighten up in their throats and shoulders and in other areas associated with breathing. String players tend to tighten up in their wrists and hands.

I want you to identify the places where you hold your tension when you're under extreme pressure. Which of your muscles tighten when you're bracing for impending danger? These are your *key muscles*, the ones you need to keep relaxed in order to perform well. Please check those muscles in the box below.

YOUR KEY MUSCLES

❑ Neck	❑ Left Shoulder	❑ Left Hand
❑ Jaw	❑ Right Shoulder	❑ Right Hand
❑ Throat	❑ Left Arm	❑ Back
❑ Face	❑ Right Arm	❑ Legs

THE MENTAL EFFECTS OF STRESS

As you may have noticed, funny things happen in our minds under stress. Usually everything speeds up. And the faster your mind goes, the less efficient it is, and the more scattered your thoughts become. Before you know it, you're on the road to memory lapses, confusion, and major problems in focusing your attention.

> *You may judge yourself more harshly under pressure than you would a friend.*

Think about the piece of music you struggle with most. Does your mind spin with a thousand unnecessary thoughts, questions, and suggestions before you sound the first note? A degree of inner dialogue may be necessary for beginners, but experienced performers can do better without it. You did all that repetition in your practice and rehearsal; it's in your muscle memory. You can trust your ability to do it without thinking in words.

Another common manifestation of stress is *self-criticism*. Under pressure, you may judge yourself more harshly than you would a friend or colleague. Remember some of your worst performances, recalling specific insults you've hurled at yourself. Aren't your best performances associated with more mental quiet, and the rest with much more of that abusive noise?

Stress can bring on negative thought patterns. These fall into three categories: *Doomsday Thinking, Weird Thinking,* and *Obsessing about Results.*

Before consequential events, you may engage in Doomsday Thinking, in which you consider the ultimate results in the worst possible terms. You haven't even started to perform and you may think: "I'm going to blow this entire concert." And then you imagine yourself doing just that. Under extreme pressure, you might jump to irrational, even frightening, conclusions. Of course this just adds more stress.

Weird Thinking includes all the strange things that may hit you under stressful circumstances. An oboist may harbor the irrational fear that side keys will start falling off the instrument during her solo. A pianist might imagine himself hitting the low notes of a concerto so hard that the whole piano comes crashing down. I could go on and on, but I don't want to put ideas into your head.

Obsessing about Results, you may put pressure on yourself to achieve certain outcomes. You may say to yourself: "I've *got* to do well," or "I *have* to get this job." This will only make things worse.

Stress can also cause a number of *attentional problems*, which take your focus away from your performance to other times and places. For example, you may become hypersensitive to internal conditions. You may remark to yourself: "Gee, I never noticed that sensation in my knee." But if you are playing the viola, who cares about your knee? It's irrelevant.

Your concentration may leave the present and your mind may jump forward, to an upcoming difficult part, or backward, to an earlier mistake. Or your mind may wander outside your current time or place altogether. In the middle of a piano trio performance, for example, you may realize that you are hungry, as in: "I wonder what's in the fridge? I think I'm out of milk." Your next thought may be: "Yikes, I missed my entrance."

> *The ability to deftly switch between left and right brain is the critical process.*

Perhaps you become more self-conscious and aware of other people. Your focus goes outside yourself to audience members, judges, fellow performers, concert hall ushers—anyone whose approval you crave. During rests and pauses between movements, you may even squint out at these people, searching their facial expressions and body language for clues to their opinion. This takes your attention away from the task-relevant process of doing what it takes to perform well.

As overwhelming as this may all seem, it's not that complicated. It's all about the *left brain* versus the *right brain*. Here goes.

The left brain is where we think in words: with running commentary, analyses, and judgments. Your left brain may be useful when you're learning a piece or a specific technique, but it can be a major obstacle to the mental quiet necessary for Optimal Performance.

The right brain is where we feel correct movements, hear beautiful sounds, and picture ourselves doing well. Our flowing movements originate in this quieter half of the brain. Rather than dissecting things into smaller pieces to be examined for differences, the right brain perceives similarities and wholes. Although the right brain is not best for certain types of learning (such as algebra and definitions), it *is* ideal for Optimal Performance and mandatory for Peak Performance.

For performing artists, the critical process is developing the ability to deftly switch between left and right brain, according to various musical demands. Those who don't build this all-important flexibility tend to get stuck. More on this topic later in the book.

So here you are. You understand how stress can affect performers. Now you're ready to address how pressure affects *you* in particular. Fasten your safety belt, take a deep breath, and smile—you're about to embark on a true adventure. It's going to be exciting. All you need to do is just follow along. I challenge you to understand this material, do the recommended exercises, and watch your talent truly take off. *You will learn how to perform so much better than you've been doing, as you will soon see.* For now, just turn the page.

4. The Seven Essential Skills for Optimal Performance

What Your Scores Mean and How to Improve Them

B Y THIS POINT you've completed and scored the Artist's Performance Survey. You've made a Before tape. And we've covered the basics of how stress works. It's time now to turn to your Artist's Performance Survey scores and find out what they can tell you about your own unique mix of strengths and weaknesses. Your scores tie directly into the seven basic skill areas essential to performance success.

As you go through the following material, consider each of your scores as a first approximation. Once you've understood what it indicates, if any given score does not seem accurate, you can change it accordingly. You know yourself better than anyone else does, and certainly better than any survey can tabulate. So make sure that your scores truly reflect your current performance tendencies.

The seven essential skill areas into which your scores are grouped are: *Determination, Poise, Mental Outlook, Emotional Approach, Attention, Concentration, and Resilience.* These factors integrally support what you do and how well you do it.

DETERMINATION

Determination is critical to every human endeavor. Your inner drive, the relative importance of performing in your life, and the strength of your resolve to do your best—all these elements come together to bring you closer to your dreams. So, how determined are you? Circle your Artist's Performance Survey scores below.

	LOW								MID-RANGE									HIGH
Intrinsic	20	25	30	35	40	45	50	55	60	65	70	75	80	85	90	95	100	
Motivation	Unclear Goals														Driven from Within			
Commitment	20	25	30	35	40	45	50	55	60	65	70	75	80	85	90	95	100	
	Other Interests															Committed		
Will to	20	25	30	35	40	45	50	55	60	65	70	75	80	85	90	95	100	
Succeed	Unimportant																Strong	

Intrinsic Motivation

Intrinsic Motivation measures your inner sense of purpose. The higher your score, the more you feel driven from within to achieve your own highest aspirations. High scores are often found in performers who are closely in touch with their motives. They may even use spiritual terms to express their love of music and their passion for sharing their gifts. Such feelings run deep.

> *Some performers may even use spiritual terms to express their love of music.*

A mid-range score in Intrinsic Motivation would suggest that your goals, though somewhat established, may need further clarification. A low score usually points to an inner drive that is stalled or perhaps just burned out. In this case there is a real need to set specific goals, or at least revisit the ones you have. Make sure that your goals are current, accurate, and inspiring. If they are not, don't worry; help is on the way.

Once again, if your score in this or any other category does not seem to be correct, please change it accordingly.

Commitment

The Commitment category measures where you place performing among your priorities and goals. A high score indicates that performing is the most critical part of your life. At this moment, it may be more important to you than your family, friends, faith, significant other, hobbies, and so forth. It's the top priority.

A mid-range score in Commitment may indicate that you equate performing with one or more other elements in your life, or place less importance on it. You value your performing, but there are other aspects of your life that are also significant. That is called balance, and that's just fine.

If your Commitment score is low, though, there may be things going on in your life right now that require more of your time, attention, and interest. This score is not a value judgment; you are the only one who can determine the balance of priorities in your life and make decisions accordingly.

Performers often ask if a Commitment score of 95 or 100 is too high. That's not for me to say. It depends on where you are in your life and career. What, if any, immediate familial or financial responsibilities must you reconcile with your performing dreams? Are you satisfied? Are you happy? Is there balance in your life? These questions are worth asking, whatever your score.

> At this moment, performing may be a top priority.

A red flag, however, would be a combination of high Commitment and low Intrinsic Motivation. It would suggest that although performing is critical in your life, you feel a lack of urgency or purpose from within. You may have lost your inner drive. Goal-setting can provide a real solution to this predicament.

Will to Succeed

Success often requires everything you've got. If you're not invested in your pursuit, you're not going to get very far. Do you intend to attain your dreams? Your Will to Succeed is your resolve to achieve your best. High scores go to performers with an intense zeal to accomplish their goals against all odds. They understand that obstacles and challenging times are inevitable in the performing arts, and that very few people make it to the top without strong conviction.

A mid-range score indicates that you may have lost your eagerness to succeed or are temporarily out of touch with it. New love relationships, family events, personal crises, and other life changes can lower your Will to Succeed. A bad audition or performance, or a string of them, can also lower your score in this category. Some upheavals need only be temporary detours, while others may prompt a thoughtful consideration of shifting options. Life happens.

Once again, having clear goals will help you stay on track. Even those with high scores in the three Determination categories should find the following section on goal-setting strategies to be beneficial.

Set Your Sights on Your Dreams

Dreams can be magical. They will be a source of inspiration to you during the work that lies ahead. If you invest your dreams with true belief in your abilities, they can help you realize your full potential and come to know a deep sense of meaning in your work.

> *Envision what you would truly love.*

Are your dreams in mind? Do you know what you're shooting for? The less vivid your dreams, the more difficult it will be to sustain the intense desire that is required to achieve worthwhile results. Hazy mental pictures produce hazy results. Without destinations in mind, all you'll see are the obstacles in your way.

Your choice of dreams is critical. What would you truly love to accomplish before you are done performing? What is in your heart? All things are possible, but if you don't believe in your dreams, no one else will. Envision what you would truly love, beyond any restrictions or self-imposed limitations. For dreams to work, they must deeply inspire you. It's got to be worth the journey. So open up your realm of possibilities. Fantasize a little bit; expand your envelope. Let your imagination run free.

In clarifying your biggest dream— your *Ultimate Dream*—you need to take into account other significant aspects of your life, now and in the future. There is nothing wrong with taking some time, a few days even, to consider thoughtfully your Ultimate Dream in the context of your life as a whole. I suggest that you consult with signifi-

> *Follow your bliss. Find where it is and don't be afraid to follow it.*
> —JOSEPH CAMPBELL

cant others, such as family members, who may figure prominently in your plans—not to mention your mother-in-law.

You may yearn to follow in the footsteps of your teacher, for example, and sit under the spotlight as part of a well-known string quartet. If so, consider your teacher's life beyond her professional status. How much money does she earn? How much free time does she have? Does she leave a family behind when she's away on tour? Look at a typical day in her life. Does it look good to you? Will it still look good to you in ten years?

Once your dreams are fully formed in your mind, write them down in the box below. By committing them to paper, you are moving toward making each of them into a reality.

Hundreds of studies have proved the effectiveness of using goals to achieve significant results. The human brain is a goal-seeking mechanism. It functions best with a progression of clearly envisioned targets. If you're a highly successful artist, you understand that all along the road to realizing your dreams you must know precisely where you're headed.

TIME	GOAL
Ultimate Dream	_____
Long-Term	_____
Intermediate	_____
Short-Term	_____

Making It Happen

It's time now to formulate a functional success strategy. The process is designed to help you clarify and accomplish short-term, intermediate, and long-term goals on the path to making your Ultimate Dream come true. All you need to do is follow along and fill in the blanks. As you do, you'll learn the process and see how it works. You can do it! Here's how.

> *Nothing happens unless first a dream.*
> —CARL SANDBURG

No matter how talented you are, the chances are good that attaining your dreams will take time and effort. What you need to do is break the job down into manageable parts, into smaller, distinct goals that will serve as landmarks on your journey. There are three types of these: *Outcome Goals, Process Goals,* and *Practice Goals.*

OUTCOME GOALS

You've written down your Ultimate Dream. Now focus on the last logical step right before achieving it. It may be several years away, but what would need to happen one step away from achieving your Ultimate Dream that will set you up to reach that final goal? Once you've got that, you'll continue to work backward in a logical progression.

If you're going to sing a leading role at a major opera house in ten years, what will you need to be doing in five years, on your way there? You're probably going to need leading roles with some regional houses or companies after winning some professional auditions. Those usually follow successful

> *You are never given*
> *a wish without also*
> *being given the power to*
> *make it come true.*
> *You may have to work*
> *for it however.*
> —RICHARD BACH

auditions for apprentice positions. Got the idea? Continue to fill in the Outcome Goals, working step by step back to your one-month, short-term goal. Goals need to be specific and tangible, objective, and measurable. You either passed the jury or not. You either signed the contract or someone else did.

Your Outcome Goals should also be reasonable and challenging. If they're not reasonable, you may work hard for a few weeks and then give up after failing several times, thinking that there is little chance of ever getting there anyway. There is nothing you cannot accomplish, but there is the element of time to consider. Whatever Outcome Goals you set, just make sure you give yourself a reasonable amount of time to get there.

> *Great things are not*
> *something accidental,*
> *but certainly must*
> *be willed.*
> —VINCENT VAN GOGH

The Outcome Goals need to be inspiring. They are the sparks that light your way. They have to be something worth striving for. They have to be worth the energy they will require.

If not, you'll lose interest and become bored with the process and complacent about early accomplishments. You'll fall off the path before reaching longer-term goals. There is a saying in race-car driving: "If you don't scare yourself at least once a lap, you're not driving fast enough." Make your goal markers really exciting, so they capture and hold your interest.

Continue to fill in the Outcome Goals, working all the way back to a one-month goal that's in line with all your subsequent goals. Make sure that each goal makes sense as part of a step-by-step path that logically leads you from wherever you are to reaching your dream. Can you see yourself taking each of those steps? I hope so.

TIME	OUTCOME GOALS	PROCESS GOALS
Three Months	_____	_____
		_____
		_____
One Month	_____	_____
		_____
		_____

PROCESS GOALS

Now you're sure *what* you clearly intend to accomplish; you've just mapped it out in a logical step-by-step progression. It's time to move on to Process Goals, in which you spell out *how* you plan to achieve your Outcome Goals.

Each Outcome Goal will have several Process Goals. Whether they be technical, physical, or mental in nature, Process Goals are the functional means for achieving your intended results. Like the Outcome Goals, the Process Goals need to be reasonable yet challenging. Unlike Outcome Goals, you'll fill them in from the bottom up, starting with the present and working chronologically forward from there.

> *What things do you need to accomplish in the next few weeks?*

If you are going to have a successful jury or recital in one month, what things do you need to accomplish in the next few weeks? Those things constitute your Process Goals for that Outcome.

Once you plan the logical sequence of Process steps to be achieved as goals, they can begin leading you to your Outcome Goals. Fill in as many Process Goals as you can, keeping in mind that you may not know what the Process Goals will be for the longer-term Outcome Goals until you get closer to them.

PRACTICE GOALS

After the *what* and the *how* goals, the last step is to set Practice Goals: the tangible *structure* for achieving each of your Process Goals. You can think of your Practice Goals as a daily To-Do list that will help focus your practicing on tangible results. This way, you won't waste a minute wandering mindlessly around your studio practice room. You will keep your attention trained on your most immediate concerns.

There may be several Practice Goals for each Process Goal. Practice Goals are more specific and detailed than the Process Goals; they need to outline the exact number of repetitions and amount of time allocated each day to attain each Process Goal. This may sound like a lot, but be assured that it's probably much less work than you already do. It's much more efficient.

> *Think of your practice goals as a daily To-Do list.*

Write out how you plan to allocate your time. For example, you may choose to work thirty minutes a day, five days a week, for one month; or twenty minutes, twice a week, for six months. Resist expecting too much; know your threshold for frustration and avoid it. Patience is key. Mastery of each goal or skill will take you a minimum of twenty-one days.

TIME	PROCESS GOALS	PRACTICE GOALS
One Month	_____	_____
	_____	_____
	_____	_____
One Week	_____	_____
	_____	_____
	_____	_____

REWARDS

As optimistic as I am, I have to acknowledge that in the performing arts, as in life, there are variables outside our control. You may prepare beautifully for your Weill Recital Hall debut. You may give an Optimal—even Peak—Performance. For you, it's a magical evening. Unfortunately, the critic reviewing the concert had a fight with his wife that afternoon, which he followed up with spicy food at the new restaurant down the block. In a terrible mood, he suffered with indigestion through your entire performance. So you get panned in the paper the next day. Some things are just outside your control and you need to accept that fact.

> *Recognize and celebrate your progress.*

Despite such detours on your way, you need always to recognize and celebrate your progress. Plan to give yourself a specific and tangible reward for attaining each Process Goal that you set. A principle of psychology is that what gets reinforced gets replayed. Before attaining the goal, know what that reward is going to be.

> *What gets reinforced gets repeated.*

For example, your Process Goal may be that you play well in a master class. So, if you play well, reward yourself whether the teacher says so or not. Give yourself a present of some kind: a reminder of what you've achieved. Make it something that will last (not a doughnut). Get something you can afford, whether it's a T-shirt or coffee mug or necklace. Make it fun and make it special. You deserve it. To get started, move to the box below and jot down what reward you'll give yourself for accomplishing your one-month and three-month Process Goals.

TIME	PROCESS GOALS	REWARDS
Three Months	_____	_____
	_____	_____
One Month	_____	_____
	_____	_____
	_____	_____

Now you understand how the strategy works. Now you're ready to put these skills into practice. If you're still not sure what your Process Goal might be, the first exercise may help.

POISE

We all know *Poise* when we see it. It looks great, and as you may know from experience, it feels great. It seems to come "naturally" to some fortunate performers, to happen as if by magic. But take the quality of Poise apart and you'll learn that it comprises tangible elements: your reaction to pressure and your ability to control your energy levels.

Performing well takes a certain amount of energy. Rather than describe this heightened state as *nervousness,* we will use *Activation,* a much more helpful term. Activation is the sum of your mental and physical energies in different performance circumstances. It's important to pinpoint the energy levels at which you perform well and in three distinct arenas: rehearsals, performances and auditions.

	LOW						MID-RANGE							HIGH			
Optimal	20	25	30	35	40	45	50	55	60	65	70	75	80	85	90	95	100
Activation	Best When Calm													Best When Up			
Rehearsal	20	25	30	35	40	45	50	55	60	65	70	75	80	85	90	95	100
Activation	Relaxed in Rehearsals													Up or Anxious			
Performance	20	25	30	35	40	45	50	55	60	65	70	75	80	85	90	95	100
Activation	Relaxed in Performance													Up or Anxious			
Audition	20	25	30	35	40	45	50	55	60	65	70	75	80	85	90	95	100
Activation	Relaxed in Auditions													Up or Anxious			

Optimal Activation

Your Optimal Activation is one of the most important scores in your Artist's Performance Survey. It identifies the energy level that accompanies your best performances. A high score indicates that you perform well when you're *up*: positively excited about your music and performing in the spotlight.

A mid-range score suggests that you perform well when your Activation level is somewhere in between being pumped and totally calm. A low score in Optimal Activation means that you perform your best when you're very relaxed. We will explore your Optimal Activation in greater depth later on.

Rehearsal Activation

Your Rehearsal Activation score indicates your energy level in most rehearsals and practice situations. How do you feel? High scores are found in performers who are either very anxious or just really up. On your first day on the job with a major symphony, for example, you're likely to be very excited—and there's nothing wrong with that.

It's more usual, however, to have a mid-range score in this category, indicating that you are neither too up nor too calm during rehearsal and practice sessions. This is just fine. Maybe you've been with your orchestra for a while, and another stellar *Nutcracker's* not going to make your day.

A low Rehearsal Activation score suggests that you may be very relaxed. Are you too mellow? If your stand partner has to wake you up three bars before your solo entrance, you'll benefit later in the book from techniques that will help you raise your Activation level at will.

Performance Activation

Your score in the Performance Activation category is an indicator of your energy level when performing in formal contexts. The score reflects how you feel on these occasions, especially at the point when you're just about to begin. High scores are found in artists who suffer with extreme anxiety as well as in those who genuinely enjoy the power of *high positive energy*. I've known many successful artists and athletes who benefited from this approach

A mid-range score in this category could reflect steady, consistent energy in the middle range. Remember, though, that this score is an average. It could also indicate that you experience extreme high and low energy levels in different performing contexts. You may be way up for some things and way down for others.

Low scores in Performance Activation mean either that you are very calm in most performances or that you are consciously suppressing vital energy. Are you just low-key by temperament or are you trying dutifully to follow the standard advice to "just relax" for important events?

Audition Activation

When was the last time you performed before a judging audience, as in a jury, competition, or audition? Does the mere thought send a shiver up your spine? High scores in Audition Activation are usually found in performers who tend to struggle in these critically assessed and consequential situations. If this describes you, you're far from doomed; you can learn to use that high energy to win competitions, pass juries, and get great jobs. Keep reading.

As in Performance Activation, a mid-range score in Audition Activation may indicate one of two things. Either your energy level is consistently moderate or you swing between two extremes. You need to ask yourself which of these describes how you feel in most auditions.

A low score in Audition Activation could point to one or more different factors. This category may not apply to you. Maybe you have a tenured position and haven't auditioned in years. Or you may have a very relaxed approach to these events and take them in stride. Perhaps you've failed in a number of auditions, in which case your energy has probably been sapped. You may still have that spark, but you're doing everything you can to suppress the energy that comes with it.

	LOW							MID-RANGE							HIGH	
Performance under Pressure	20	25	30	35	40	45	50	55	60	65	70	75	80	85	90	95	100
	Sabotaged															Optimal
Ability to Activate	20	25	30	35	40	45	50	55	60	65	70	75	80	85	90	95	100
	Difficulty Getting Up												Able to Raise Energy
Ability to Deactivate	20	25	30	35	40	45	50	55	60	65	70	75	80	85	90	95	100
	Difficulty Relaxing												Able to Lower Energy

Performance under Pressure

Your Performance under Pressure score reflects your perception of how well you perform in stressful circumstances. A high score indicates that you've probably found successful strategies for dealing with performance pressure and that you know how to function well under stress. In fact, you may even get a kick out of it, and regard high-pressure performances as challenging opportunities.

Mid-range scores in Performance under Pressure would suggest mixed results in stressful situations. How well you do in any given situation may depend upon a number of internal and external circumstances. This score could also indicate that you have developed certain Optimal Performance skills that are somewhat effective for you in certain situations.

Just as some of us know what Poise feels like, every one of us is familiar with the horrible agony of crashing and burning in public. If you scored low in this category, you've experienced this too often. It doesn't have to be this way. You can learn to regulate your Activation levels under pressure.

Ability to Activate

It takes energy to perform. Your Ability to Activate score indicates how well you get yourself up when you need to, especially when you're fatigued. A high score means that you're able to rise to virtually any occasion. If you have a mid-range score, sometimes you're able to raise your energy adequately and at other times, not. It would depend upon the circumstances and how you are feeling.

If your score in Ability to Activate is low, you may have trouble raising your energy when required. You may find the process of *Centering Up,* which I'll explain later, to be of real value. If you're like most performers, however, your more frequent and pressing concern is not raising your energy, but lowering it.

Ability to Deactivate

The Ability to Deactivate is the ability to relax when needed. Your score in this category reflects what you perceive to be your capacity to control your so-called nervous energy. High scores are found in performers who know how to bring their Activation down to Optimal levels.

A mid-range score in this category indicates that you are sometimes able to lower your Activation effectively and at other times, not. It would depend on the circumstances.

A Low score in Ability to Deactivate suggests that bringing your nervousness under control is difficult for you. Believe me, I can still remember how much panic I felt in the days when I wrestled with my inability to control my nerves. It was a horrible feeling that I'll never forget. But there's hope on the way.

Find Poise

Optimal Performance is founded on being able to perform well, not only at a precise energy point but across a wide band of potential energy levels: your Optimal Activation range.

Consider some of your recent Optimal Performances, occasions on which you performed very well, though not necessarily at Peak Performance levels. You'd give yourself an *A* but probably not an *A+*. List at least three such instances below, including the specific occasion, location, month, and year. For each of these, indicate your Activation level on a scale from 20 to 100. You'd be asleep at 20, in the mid-range at 60, and bouncing off the wall at 100.

OPTIMAL PERFORMANCES

EVENT	LOCATION	DATE	ACTIVATION LEVEL
_____	_____	_____	_____
_____	_____	_____	_____
_____	_____	_____	_____
_____	_____	_____	_____
_____	_____	_____	_____

Below, circle each of the Activation levels that accompanied your Optimal Performances. For example, if the Activation levels that accompanied recent Optimal Performances were 45, 60, and 65, it would look like this.

	LOW	MID-RANGE	HIGH

Optimal Activation   20 25 30 35 40 [(45) 50 55 (60) (65)]70 75 80 85 90 95 100
Best When Calm   Best When Up

	LOW	MID-RANGE	HIGH

Optimal Activation   20 25 30 35 40 45 50 55 60 65 70 75 80 85 90 95 100
Best When Calm   Best When Up

Now refer to your Artist's Performance Survey to find your Optimal Activation score. Circle that number as well. On the line above the circled Activation levels, mark the lowest and highest points with brackets. The brackets will show your Optimal Activation range. In the example, the range would go from 45 to 65.

The broader your Optimal Activation range, the better. Breadth allows you to do well in different situations and at varying energy levels. Performers who have a wide range enjoy a sense of freedom and flexibility. They're not restricted by the need to be at a specific point or narrow band of energy.

With this in mind, you may want to revise your list of Optimal Performances to include other times, when lower or higher Activation levels resulted in success. If your Optimal Activation range is on the low side, think about including past events or occasions on which you were really up and you did well. And vice versa.

Bracket your Optimal Activation range on the line below. Then refer to your survey scores for Rehearsal Activation, Performance Activation, and Audition Activation and circle them below.

	LOW							MID-RANGE							HIGH	
Optimal	20	25	30	35	40	45	50	55	60	65	70	75	80	85	90	95 100
Activation	Best When Calm												Best When Up			
Rehearsal	20	25	30	35	40	45	50	55	60	65	70	75	80	85	90	95 100
Activation	Relaxed in Rehearsals												Up or Anxious			
Performance	20	25	30	35	40	45	50	55	60	65	70	75	80	85	90	95 100
Activation	Relaxed in Performance												Up or Anxious			
Audition	20	25	30	35	40	45	50	55	60	65	70	75	80	85	90	95 100
Activation	Relaxed in Auditions												Up or Anxious			

How does it look? Are you spending the majority of your time at or near the energy levels that produce your Optimal? Yes? No? Any light-bulbs flashing yet?

Let's look at some classic examples showing how the placement of energy in these four related categories can set up Suboptimal or Optimal

Performances. Please find the closest approximation to your pattern of scores in the following three examples.

	LOW						MID-RANGE								HIGH	
Optimal *Activation*	20	25	30	35	40	45	50[(55)	(60)	(65)]70	75	80	85	90	95	100	
	Best When Calm												Best When Up			
Rehearsal *Activation*	20	25	30	35	(40)	45	50	55	60	65	70	75	80	85	90	95 100
	Relaxed in Rehearsals												Up or Anxious			
Performance *Activation*	20	25	30	35	40	(45)	50	55	60	65	70	75	80	85	90	95 100
	Relaxed in Performance												Up or Anxious			
Audition *Activation*	20	25	30	35	40	45	50	55	60	65	70	75	80	(85)	90	95 100
	Relaxed in Auditions												Up or Anxious			

Many performers tend to be more relaxed in rehearsals and more nervous in auditions. That's fairly standard. In the example above, the Optimal Activation range [(55 to 65)] would indicate that you perform better in the mid-range of energy. Low scores for Rehearsal Activation (40) and Performance Activation (45) may indicate that you have extensive performing experience. You're very relaxed in rehearsals and even calm in most performances.

But the Audition Activation score (85) shows significantly higher Activation levels in auditions. This is usually indicative of extreme anxiety. Accustomed to performing at lower energy levels over a period of time, you may find it a real shock to perform an audition at this unfamiliar, high-energy level.

In this case, your range needs to expand to allow for Optimal Performances at a greater variety of energy levels. It would also help if the three Activation levels were closer together, namely, somewhat more Activated in rehearsals and performances and less so in auditions. Why? So that you can become accustomed to performing more of the time at or near the energy level where you perform well. The exercises and drills that I'll show you later will help you do that.

The next example represents another pattern that often results in Suboptimal Performance.

	LOW	MID-RANGE	HIGH →
Optimal Activation	20 25 30 35 [(40) (45) 50 (55)]60 65 70 75 80 85 90 95 100 Best When Calm		Best When Up
Rehearsal Activation	20 25 30 35 40 (45) 50 55 60 65 70 75 80 85 90 95 100 Relaxed in Rehearsals		Up or Anxious
Performance Activation	20 25 30 35 40 45 50 55 60 65 70 (75) 80 85 90 95 100 Relaxed in Performance		Up or Anxious
Audition Activation	20 25 (30) 35 40 45 50 55 60 65 70 75 80 85 90 95 100 Relaxed in Auditions		Up or Anxious

Your Optimal Activation range [(40 to 55)] is on the low side, meaning that you perform best when you're relatively calm and relaxed. Your Rehearsal Activation (45) is within this range, suggesting that you're fairly mellow in practice sessions and probably perform well in rehearsals.

The Performance Activation would indicate that performance situations cause your energy to shift to a much higher level (75). Since this appears to be outside the Optimal range, it is probably not a desired effect. You may feel as though you can manage, but you are always flirting in some way with disaster. Audiences may not notice anything amiss, but you may feel that you're just barely hanging on.

Your Audition Activation is low, but perhaps you're afraid that the adrenaline of an audition will send you over the top. So in auditions, you try to suppress your energy to a low level (30). You may feel somewhat safer as a result, but the more that energy is pushed down, the farther it gets from your Optimal range. Audition judges often regard this type of performance as flat or bland: in a word, *boring*.

The next example shows another pattern that frequently causes problems for many performers.

	LOW	MID-RANGE	HIGH →
Optimal Activation	20 25 30 35 40 [(45) 50 (55)]60 65 70 75 80 85 90 95 100 Best When Calm		Best When Up
Rehearsal Activation	20 25 30 35 40 45 50 55 60 (65) 70 75 80 85 90 95 100 Relaxed in Rehearsals		Up or Anxious
Performance Activation	20 25 30 35 40 45 50 55 60 65 70 (75) 80 85 90 95 100 Relaxed in Performance		Up or Anxious
Audition Activation	20 25 30 35 40 45 50 55 60 65 70 75 80 85 (90) 95 100 Relaxed in Auditions		Up or Anxious

Your Optimal Activation range is narrow and on the low side [(45 to 55)], indicating your need to be very relaxed in order to perform well. But this is not a realistic expectation, in light of the fact that even your Rehearsal Activation (65) drives you beyond your Optimal range. It gets worse. Performances send your energy and most likely your anxiety higher still (75). In auditions, your energy spirals up and out of control (90). This cannot feel good or produce anything close to your Optimal.

Again, the solution to this pattern involves a combination of approaches. Your Optimal Activation range needs to expand, especially in the upper range. You can do this by practicing at increasingly higher Activation levels while also developing your ability to *Center Down*.

This last example shows an Optimal approach employed by many successful performers.

	LOW	MID-RANGE	HIGH
Optimal Activation	20 25 30 35 40 45 50 [(55) 60 65 70 75 (80)] 85 90 95 100 Best When Calm Best When Up		
Rehearsal Activation	20 25 30 35 40 45 (50) 55 60 65 70 75 80 85 90 95 100 Relaxed in Rehearsals Up or Anxious		
Performance Activation	20 25 30 35 40 45 50 55 60 65 (70) 75 80 85 90 95 100 Relaxed in Performance Up or Anxious		
Audition Activation	20 25 30 35 40 45 50 55 60 65 70 (75) 80 85 90 95 100 Relaxed in Auditions Up or Anxious		

It indicates a wide Optimal Activation range (from 55 to 80). The Rehearsal Activation (50) is on the more relaxed side, as may be expected. The Performance Activation (70) and Audition Activation (75) are progressively more activated. All the levels are nevertheless within the Optimal range.

Once you understand what you need to do with your Activation levels to perform Optimally, you can then learn to lower or raise your energy whenever you choose. Moving energy down or up is not as difficult, or as esoteric, as you may think. The technique you will learn for moving your energy is called *Centering*. Once you master the Centering process, it will take you only a few seconds to lower or raise your energy at will. You'll learn to Center Down and Center Up. Then you'll be able to practice per-forming within your Optimal Activation range all the time. It will become a habit. That's how this process works. How's that sound? You can do it. Really!

Learn to Center

Centering is a focusing strategy that helps performers channel energy productively under extreme circumstances. Dr. Robert Nideffer designed the technique in the seventies. I have adapted it for the specific needs of performing artists.

Centering has great applications for performing artists looking to adjust their Activation levels to within their Optimal range. It's dramati-cally effective, and with practice, it can be amazingly quick. Once you master Centering, you will literally be able to become more Poised in a matter of seconds. You will be able to raise or lower your Activation levels whenever you choose.

The Centering process also helps you make the important shift from left to right brain immediately before you begin performing. As I mentioned earlier, the brain's left hemisphere is where we talk to our-selves in words, where our fears, worries, and doubts are announced. It's responsible for all the instructions, criticism, and running commentary artists tend to "hear" under high stress. The more you think, the faster it goes.

As your left brain speeds up, your thinking becomes more scattered and probably more negative. The faster it goes, the less you're focused, the tighter your muscles, and the more negative the outcomes you envi-sion. This left-brain approach usually sets up Suboptimal Performances. Again, with Centering practice, this important shift from left to right brain can be made within a few seconds.

The right brain is a wonderful place from which to perform; it's much quieter and more focused than the left brain. Its Alpha waves are slower and more concentrated. The right brain is also where you can best imagine sights, feelings, and sounds. Working from the right brain, you can picture what you want to do, get a feeling for how you are going to do it, and hear the sound that you'd like to create. All three are good options because all three focus on *Process*. This sets you up to per-form your best. The first type of Centering you will learn is known as *Centering Down*.

CENTERING DOWN

You can practice Centering Down while sitting with your hands relaxed in your lap. Or you can stand with your head tilted slightly down, your feet shoulder-width apart, and your arms and hands hanging heavy at your sides. Either way, find a balanced position. If you prefer, you can adopt either of these poses with your chin resting gently on your chest.

FORM YOUR CLEAR INTENTION In the Centering Down process, there is a "going in" and a "coming out." You start the process by forming a clear idea of what you intend to do when you "come out" of the Centering. Focus your attention on exactly what you will accomplish.

You *form your clear intention* by stating your goal in precise terms. You might say: "I am going to practice minor-key arpeggios for the next twenty minutes," or "I'm going to play the Act II solos well tonight." For right now, your clear intention might be: "I'm going to learn how to Center Down." That would be a good place to begin.

PICK YOUR FOCUS POINT The second thing to do is to *pick your focus point*. Direct your focus to a specific location in your performance space, some distance away, where you will channel the extra energy that accompanies most stressful performances and adverse circumstances.

It's important that you choose a focus point below your eye level. Why? If it's higher than eye level, your mind will tend to go into left-brain thinking. Looking down, or having your eyes closed, is much more conducive to right-brain and Alpha waves. It will allow your energy to flow effortlessly downward to your focus point. Did you ever notice how this helps baseball pitchers on the elevated mound to throw fast balls down to their catchers? It does.

Again, your focus point is a precise spot. It could be on a music stand or at the back of the auditorium. Just make sure it is lower than eye level. Narrow your scope of attention onto this tangible focus point.

CLOSE YOUR EYES, FOCUS ON YOUR BREATHING After choosing your focus point, close your eyes and pay close attention to your breathing. Eventually you will be able to focus on your breathing with your eyes open, looking down, with a "soft focus." For now, however, practice with your eyes closed.

Start to breathe *slowly* and *deeply* throughout your entire torso. Breathe *in through your nose* and *out through your mouth*. As you inhale, allow your ribs, back, abdomen, and upper body to fill gently with air. As you do so, pay attention only to your breathing. Do this for three to seven breaths, or as many as it takes for you to become fully mindful of your breathing.

You may find it helpful at first to practice breathing in a prone position (lying with your back flat on the floor). This will obviously place your focus point somewhere on the ceiling. Make sure to cast your gaze downward before you close your eyes.

SCAN FOR EXCESS TENSION AND RELEASE IT Under high stress, many performers get overloaded and don't pay attention to muscle tension. It can get progressively worse. That's why it's so critical in stressful circumstances to continually monitor your Key Muscles. The simple process of checking them leads to releasing the tension.

As you continue to breathe fully, begin to scan your body for tension, especially in your key muscles. On each inhale, check one area. Then breathe out any tension you find on the exhale. Continue to do this for three to seven breaths, until all your key muscles are relatively relaxed and ready to function well.

FIND YOUR CENTER Concentration is like a still pond. Each thought that you have is like a pebble splashing into the water. Many performers in left-brain states spray their concentration ponds with gravel. To be Centered, though, you need to quiet your mind, if only briefly, before you begin performing. As the instructions on my Japanese hibachi set read: "Before attempting to assemble, attain peace of mind."

Now it's time to locate your Center. It's approximately two inches below your navel and two inches into your body. Pinpointing its precise location is not as important as getting out of your head and focusing your energy down, toward a place of stillness. Your Center is roughly at the center of your body, your center of gravity. Get in touch with that place. If it helps, put your hand there until you get a sense for it. Meanwhile, recognize your contact with the ground or chair. Allow yourself to feel the chair or ground as a solid, stabilizing place.

Here's another way to find your Center. Stand with your feet shoulder-width apart, hands at your sides, and knees slightly flexed. Close your eyes and make believe that there's a hula hoop around your waist. Now begin moving your hips. As you imagine the hula hoop staying up, imagine it getting smaller and smaller, but keep the rotation going. Move your hips in smaller and smaller circles, down to a tiny one, the size of a quarter. Find the center of that quarter and then drop it down about an inch. There's your Center!

Now sit down in a straight-backed chair and again try to find that point. If you need to rotate your hips again to locate it, please do so. Then sense the contact of your seat bones to the chair. Rather than pull up and away from the chair, *release* your lower back muscles to achieve more contact. If this causes you to sink down in the chair and feel compressed, tip a little bit forward on your seat bones and imagine energy moving up through your spine.

Whether you are sitting or standing, the idea is to have a solid foundation from your waist down. What happens to your center of gravity when you're under stress? It probably goes up. If you watch sopranos who get into trouble with high notes, you'll see them go up. They tend to go up on their toes and lose their base and balance. Your power comes from your Center; your solid foundation is below. You need to focus your energy downward, towards your Center.

Feel stable in your Center and stay there for three to seven breaths. Find your quiet, still point and hang out there for more and more breaths. Practice this often. You should be aware of a difference within a few days.

REPEAT YOUR PROCESS CUES Once fully at your Center for three or more breaths, then you're ready to switch from your left brain to right brain. You do this with simple, supportive directions known as *Process Cues*. For example, your Process Cue for the opening of Mendelssohn's Violin Concerto might be "smooth bowing." One that often works for wind players and vocalists is to "keep the air flowing."

Process Cues are the very directives that good teachers may have given you for years, such as "support" for singers, and "even out the shifts" for string players. These simple words and phrases are more helpful than your left brain may want to admit, especially in high-pressure performance.

Process Cues are formed with cause words rather than effect words. Effect words like "beautiful" or "passionate" are not close enough to the source or cause of producing those effects. That's why words like "support" and "flow" are so helpful. They remind you of what is important to do in the moment to produce the effects you would like to achieve.

Having found your Center, coordinate your Process Cues with your breathing: inhale, "flow," exhale, inhale, "flow," exhale. You get the idea. Do this for as long as it takes you to get into your right brain, where you can "quietly" see yourself doing the correct movements, feel yourself performing well, and hear your beautiful sound. Imagine that!

DIRECT YOUR ENERGY From your solid base, accumulate your energy at your Center. Then allow it to spin up and through your torso. Feel it rise up into your neck, open your eyes, and allow it to go out, in a flowing motion. Then narrow and intensify it, like a laser beam. Direct it at a place in the distance. We will call this spot your *focus point*.

Sense the connection between your Center and your focus point. You are ready to make your clear intention a reality. Summon your courage and trust your talent and experience. You can smile, as you let go and Go For It!

I recommend that you start out by practicing Centering three to ten times a day at first. If you do it as part of your daily routine before you warm up, practice, and perform, you will note significant changes within a week. Centering will get quicker and easier; eventually you'll be able to Center in one to three breaths.

Keep in mind, though, that the goal is not speed but true mastery of each step. Make sure that you form a clear intention, breathe properly, get your key muscles relaxed, and so forth, in as many breaths as it takes. Then, with proficiency, you can start reducing the number of breaths and time that you spend on each step.

The process is similar to driving to a friend's house in the country for the first time. Even with detailed instructions, you may have to take some U-turns, backtrack or even ask for directions. The next time you go, it's a little more direct. By the third or fourth time, you just drive straight there.

Centering will take you from the "normal" state of tight muscles and left-brain thinking to a very special state, much more suited to Optimal Performance. Like that house in the country, the more times you go there, the more familiar you become with the territory. The trip gets quick and easy.

Centering will soon become a functional part of your pre-event routine, just like tuning, stretching, or warming up. Then you can take it with you into high-pressure situations. It will feel like a trusted friend. Believe me, if you're going into adversity—and in the performing arts you very often are—you need as many friends as you can get.

When you start to practice Centering Down, it should take you between thirty seconds and two minutes. As with any learned skill, your ability to Center will improve with correct practice and repetition. If you use Centering Down as a part of your normal routine before you warm up, rehearse, or perform, you will be able to Center in ten seconds or less. When you first start practicing, though, the goal is not to see how fast you can Center, but to accomplish the task of each step in the process.

So make sure that you form a clear intention and pick your focus point. Close your eyes and focus on your breathing. Breathe out excess tension. Be at your Center. Repeat your Process Cues until you're in your right brain. Now direct your energy to your focus point. Once you sense the connection, smile. You are ready to let go and Go For It!

The following Centering Log will help guide your practice and progress in Centering Down. The Process Goal is to Center—set up for Optimal Performance—in less than ten seconds. Practice centering at least five to seven times a day for the next week.

CENTERING DOWN LOG

DATE	CLEAR INTENTION	KEY MUSCLES	PROCESS CUE	AT CENTER	NUMBER OF BREATHS	COMMENTS

MENTAL OUTLOOK

What you think is what you get. What you project for yourself has every-thing to do with how things will ultimately unfold. Your mental outlook is your mind-set leading up to and during performances. It's your cur-rent belief in your talent and abilities, how you talk to yourself while per-forming—especially when things are not going well—and how you expect your performance to turn out.

	LOW						MID-RANGE									HIGH	
Self-Confidence	20	25	30	35	40	45	50	55	60	65	70	75	80	85	90	95	100
	Doubting															Confident	
Self-Talk	20	25	30	35	40	45	50	55	60	65	70	75	80	85	90	95	100
	Negative															Positive	
Expectancy	20	25	30	35	40	45	50	55	60	65	70	75	80	85	90	95	100
	Imagine the Worst														Expect the Best		

Self-Confidence

Confidence is never static. You're either moving forward, accumulating more confidence as you go up, or backward, losing confidence as you go down. As they say in race-car driving, "there's no coasting." You're on the gas, accelerating, or on the brakes, slowing down. You're gaining or los-ing. What are *you* doing?

Your Self-Confidence score indicates how much belief you felt in your talent and training at the time you responded to the survey. "You're only as good as your last performance," goes the old cliché, so your score in this area may be only a temporary marker at best. Your score will prob-ably be high if your most recent performance went well, or low if you gave a Suboptimal Performance last time you went onstage. This cate-gory is a useful benchmark, an initial indicator with which to compare the future.

A high score in Self-Confidence can mean that you have valid rea-sons for your strong belief in your talent and abilities. It could also mean that you've been deluding yourself. Are you really that good? A third possibility is that you've learned practical ways to increase this valuable commodity.

A mid-range score in Self-Confidence opens the possibility that you may feel less than totally confident in your talent and abilities, or that your confidence wavers over time. Many performers feel this way from time to time. You may question your ability, especially during times of extreme stress or when you're feeling tired. It's amazing how your skills deteriorate when you're exhausted. A children's concert can feel like a Carnegie debut when you're fatigued.

A low Self-Confidence score suggests that you're probably selling yourself short. What about all those years you've been practicing? What about all those great concerts? How did you get into music school if you're such an inferior musician? Or was it all just a big accident?

Self-Confidence does not just happen. Many factors influence it, including the words we speak to ourselves, the mental images we form in our minds, and the repetitive actions we take in real life.

Self-Talk

Self-Talk is the nature and quality of what you say to yourself under pressure. High scores for Self-Talk are found in performers who talk to themselves in a positive and supportive way under stressful circumstances. These individuals tend to do well because they are not sabotaging their best efforts with words. If you have a high score, please continue to pat yourself on the back. As you will understand better as we go along, positive reinforcement makes a huge difference.

A mid-range Self-Talk score indicates more conditional inner dialogue; its quality depends on the situation. You're supportive and positive with your Self-Talk when your performing is going well. When it's not going well, though, you may start chewing yourself out, saying things to yourself that you'd never say to a friend or student.

If your Self-Talk score is low, welcome to the club. Working with top performers of all kinds, I've found that many, if not most, attribute their success to high personal standards. I have no problem with that. But unfortunately, sometimes when top performers fail to attain their own sometimes shockingly high expectations, they hurl harsh—often abusive—verbal attacks at themselves. This stick approach is a motivational strategy in which performers continually push themselves toward unattainable perfection.

The stick approach can and usually does backfire. Assaulted by verbal abuse, your confidence can plummet and your key muscles can lock up with tension. Suddenly you find yourself trapped in a nightmare of screaming critical voices. The "carrot" approach, on the other hand, is all about sustaining positive Self-Talk under stress. It is a strategy essential to both Optimal and Peak Performances. Stay tuned.

Expectancy

The Expectancy score rates your mind-set regarding upcoming events and how you think things are going to go. "Pollyanna" types score high in Expectancy, always anticipating that things will turn out great. Often, for these performers, things do turn out well. This is no coincidence.

If you have a mid-range score in Expectancy, you probably take a "wait and see" approach to performances. You want to see how it goes when it happens. Until then, who knows? Sometimes it'll be good, other times not; it just depends.

Low scores in Expectancy indicate a tendency to engage in Doomsday Thinking. The lower your score, the more likely you are to imagine the worst. This, of course, becomes a self-fulfilling prophecy. There is a strong correlation between your Expectancy and your performance results.

Develop an Optimal Outlook

Like so many other aspects of Optimal Performance, Self-Confidence may seem to just happen. But it doesn't work that way. You can increase your Self-Confidence in three ways: with the words you say to yourself and others, with the images you see in your mind, and with the actions you take every day. To arrive at your goals and dreams, you'll need to learn all three routes to higher Self-Confidence.

The first way is through your Self-Talk—what you say to yourself about your performance. Your words are more important than you may think. For example, if you continually say that you are having difficulty and that there is nothing you can do about it, you will tend to live a frustrated life. Your words will help to bring about those circumstances, or at least reinforce them, and help sustain the difficulty.

Improving Your Self-Talk

As you know, Self-Talk comes from the left brain, home of your worst enemies: your personal music critics, your Doomsday Thinkers, and your seventh-grade band teacher who said you'd never make it as a musician. Maybe it's time to show these folks the door because, after all, what you think is what you get.

The things you say to yourself under stress register cumulatively in your mind and deeply in your self-belief system. Since it is you speaking to yourself, you probably don't filter any of it. Your mind takes your words very seriously.

Your subconscious does not hear the word *don't*. So consider the implications of such a well-meaning instruction as "don't come in early," or of how your brain perceives "I hope I don't screw up!" To make matters worse, your subconscious unfortunately does not have a sense of humor. It believes everything you tell it, even if you think you are joking.

This does not mean that your subconscious is not powerful. In fact, it's far more powerful than your left brain and conscious mind will ever admit. Your subconscious mind is like a mushroom. It sits there in the dark ready to eat up and believe anything you feed it. Examine what you've been feeding it and monitor what you continue to reinforce. Are you like so many performers who readily agree with and quickly internalize criticism from any source, while doubting the sincerity of compliments?

> *Self trust is the first secret of success.*
> —RALPH WALDO EMERSON

The good news is that you can replace old, negative thought patterns with more helpful ones, raising your Self-Confidence in the process. Take, for example, the difference between the words *difficult* and *challenging*. These two words can produce very different outcomes. If you view a situation as difficult or hard, it will be exactly that. Since you are describing it that way to yourself or others, you are putting yourself in the position of a victim. If you think of your situation as hard and very difficult, there is little you can do about it. Who could expect you to do anything, anyway? After all, it's difficult. You are arguing for the difficulty of the situation and against your ability to remedy it.

> *Consciously or unconsciously, you always get what you expect.*
> —ROBERT ANTHONY

49

If you view your situation as a challenge, though, it becomes an opportunity to develop your abilities or prove your talent. You can argue for your talent and ability to respond to it. If you argue that it is hard, it weakens you; when you see it as an opportunity and confront it with courage, it strengthens you.

The shift in thinking, from describing a situation as difficult to characterizing it as challenging, will change what you experience. You're no longer a victim; you're in control. Perception precedes thought. What you think is what you get. The more you hold something in your mind, the more it becomes who you are and what you experience. Your experience confirms your perception. And so the circle is complete.

> *I don't believe
> in pessimism.*
> —CLINT EASTWOOD

If this is relatively new information for you, please consider reading *Psycho-Cybernetics*, by Dr. Maxwell Maltz (Prentice-Hall, 1960). Although it was written many years ago, as far as I am concerned it is the bible on Self-Talk. It's like an owner's manual for your brain. *Psycho-Cybernetics* explains how the cybernetic, or feedback, system in our minds functions to produce failure or success. The system does not care whether you win or lose; it functions the same. Although the language in the book is somewhat outdated, the basic concepts are timeless.

> *Argue for your
> limitations and sure
> enough, they're yours.*
> —RICHARD BACH

So get your instrument out or get ready to sing. You'll again perform your three repertoire selections. As you did when taping them, perform them straight through without stopping, with only a short pause between them.

When you've finished, recall what you said to yourself while performing. Take time to go through each of the pieces again in your mind, so that you can accurately capture the dialogue. You may have said things like: "Don't come in late again," "Way to go," "Nice trill," "Why does my bow always shake?" or "My rhythm sucks."

Now it's time to fill in *your* remarks. In the box below, write the exact words or phrases you "heard," especially before, during, and after difficulties.

SELF-TALK

_____

_____

_____

_____

_____

_____

Take a good look at what you wrote. Is it constructive? Would you say these things to a good friend or student? Determine whether the statements are current and accurate. If you said that you need to practice more or improve a certain aspect of your technique, those are constructive ideas. You can turn them into goals and build them into your practice structure.

In the box below, convert your negative statements to positive ones. Rather than, "don't miss that note again," you might write: "Go after it," or "Keep the air flowing." You can also challenge some of the more negative voices. Tell them what you've done to improve.

Example:

Don't come in late again ⟶ Count the rests

My bow always shakes ⟶ Stay smooth

My rhythm sucks ⟶ Write the beats over the notes.

POSITIVE STATEMENTS

_____

_____

_____

_____

_____

_____

Good job. But that's not enough. You now need to get your music out. In all the places where you said those negative things to yourself, write your new, positive statements above the notes. When you come to those points in the music, say your positive statements to yourself or out loud.

> *The person who says it cannot be done should not interrupt the person doing it.*
> —CHINESE PROVERB

Repeat this entire process as much as you need to. Weed out those negatives and plant great positives. The Process Goal of this drill is to be able to play through your three repertoire pieces hearing only encouragement and Process Cues—or best of all, experiencing right-brain quiet. Shhh!

Mental Rehearsal

In addition to his revolutionary ideas on Self-Talk, Dr. Maltz also stressed the importance of *mental imagery* in raising Self-Confidence. In the mind, an image is worth a thousand words. In your subconscious, you have stored countless visual memories in the form of mental snapshots and videos. Tucked away in your archives are not only pleasant memories, but if you're a serious musician, plenty of horror movies, too.

> *Self-image sets the boundaries of individual accomplishment.*
> —MAXWELL MALTZ

What are some of your worst performance memories? Perhaps you've suffered an embarrassing memory lapse. If you're a violinist, surely you've had a string pop at the worst time. Whatever your personal horror films, do you spend a disproportionate amount of time watching their ugliest scenes over and over?

Mental Rehearsal is an effective way to turn off those B movies. Whether they really happened or occurred only in your mind, such images can have a devastating effect on your everyday performance. Once you realize how these familiar pictures adversely affect your performance, you will probably choose to start watching better movies.

What you flash on in your mind's eye, intermittently throughout the day, over weeks and months, tends to become who you are. If you continually imagine yourself making a mistake, you will probably make it. You are the one choosing the pictures.

You are the director, the producer, and, in the end, the projectionist. If you don't like what you keep seeing, you can show a different movie. It's up to you. Oh, by the way, you also play the lead role. You're the star. You have a wonderful opportunity awaiting you, so smile.

Mental Rehearsal is one of the best techniques to use in preparing for Optimal Performance. Numerous sports psychology studies have proved the effectiveness of this technique in helping athletes perform complex skills under pressure.

If you cannot imagine yourself performing well, you have very little chance of actually doing that, especially under pressure. If you've never been able to achieve a certain goal, it may be that you have not been able to imagine yourself accomplishing it. Mental Rehearsal can pave the way for you.

When I was twelve years old someone suggested that I try Mental Rehearsal, also known as *visualization,* for my toughest springboard dives. When I tried it, all I saw were more dives, hitting the board or water wrong. Unfortunately, I stopped using visualization for the remainder of my diving career. Later, in graduate school, I was very skeptical about the technique. I downplayed it in my early work with athletes—until the time came when I had to use it.

I was working with the Mission Viejo, California, diving team two months before the 1984 Olympic trials. One of our young women platform divers—we'll call her Pam—had a bad accident. Although she was an Olympic hopeful, Pam was a long shot at best. She had never won any major competition. The Mission Viejo team

> *Artur Schnabel, the world-famous concert pianist, hated practice and seldom does practice for any length of time at the actual piano keyboard. When questioned about his small amount of practice, he said: "I practice in my head."*
>
> —MAXWELL MALTZ

had several other women who were already national and world champions, and much more likely to win one of the two spots on the U.S. Olympic team.

One day in practice, Pam was on the ten-meter platform. (Divers say the ten-meter platform is 33 feet up, but it seems like 100 feet *down*.) She was attempting a back two-and-a-half somersault in the pike position. Rather than jumping up aggressively to start the backwards rotation, she "sat back" and got off to a low, and very slow, start. After the second somersault, when she spotted her last visual reference point, she came out of the pike and reached back for the water to drop a few meters to a head-first entry.

Unfortunately, she was much lower than usual. Instead of coming out of the pike lying flat out, and dropping while rotating to vertical, Pam landed absolutely flat on her back on the water. It was painful to watch. Encountered by a human body moving at 35 miles per hour, water might as well be concrete. She seemed to bounce. We thought her back was broken.

She was immediately rushed to the team's orthopedic surgeon, who did all the X rays and tests before telling her how lucky she was. It was only soft-tissue damage; she would be black and blue and very sore for a few weeks, but there was nothing broken. Like any Olympic athlete, her next question was whether she still had a chance to make the team.

The surgeon told her that she actually might be able to dive at the Olympic trials but that she probably would not be able to practice before departing for the trials in seven weeks. Her back could not withstand the pounding of daily practices. Pam still wanted to try, though, which was extremely impressive. For divers, fears increase dramatically with every day of not throwing oneself off the 33-foot platform.

She would not be able to learn a new dive as a replacement in the meantime. If she was going to dive in the Olympic trials and have any chance of making the team, she would need to use the back two-and-a-half as one of her eight dives. She needed to do that dive and her other seven dives well if she was going to win a place on the Olympic team. Mental Rehearsal was our only option.

After she was able to get up and move around, we began her first Mental Rehearsal session in the coach's office. While the other divers were outside going through their dives, Pam was imagining herself doing her practice dives over and over. We started on the easier dives, making sure that she saw and felt them just the way she wanted them to be. Then we moved on to her tougher dives, and eventually to the back two-and-a-half. It was critical that we correct the mistake in her mind.

For the next six weeks, she imagined herself doing all her dives. Some dives, like the back two-and-a-half, required more time than others to work through. At first, she needed to go through her takeoff in slow motion to correct her tendency to sit back. Once she was able to imagine herself jumping up strongly to start the rotation properly, she saw her reference spots clearly before reaching back for the water. She then felt her body going into the water straight up and down, without making a splash. After doing the entire dive correctly in slow motion, she gradually increased the speed until she was imagining it in real time. She went through the dive repeatedly in her mind until she was doing it right every time.

The physician examined her again right before we all left for the trials in Indianapolis. The coach wanted to get there a week early, so the divers could get used to the pool and to their new visual reference points. The doctor told Pam that she could go and that she might even be able to compete, but that she would probably not be able to practice in the new pool in the final week before the trials. So we went into the training room and used one of the training tables to continue going through her eight dives just the way she intended to do them.

We did that for another week. On the day of the meet, the surgeon told her that she would be able to dive, but that she could not do any warm-up dives. She would not be able to adjust to the platform, the pool, or the new visual reference points. Imagine doing complicated platform dives in a major competition for the first time in two months, and expecting to do well. We went through all of it in fine detail in the training room.

The competition finally began. Pam got off to an amazing start. She did a great first dive, just the way she had imagined it over and over. The physician checked her back after she came out of the pool; she was okay. Then she nailed her next dive, then the next one, and the next. After the first five rounds of dives, Pam was leading the competition! It was incredible. She was ahead of all the other divers, including the current national and world champions. Neither of those two divers had missed even a day's practice in months.

Pam was the only diver in the competition, though, who had experienced only good dives in the weeks leading up to the trials. While every other diver had hit and missed dives in recent practice sessions, Pam's subconscious was aware only of hitting dive after dive after dive. It was no surprise to her, but everyone else at the pool was in shock. The large electronic board displayed the leaders' scores. If Pam hit her final three dives, she would be on her way to the Olympic Games. It was very exciting!

Unfortunately, on her sixth dive, Pam got off to a tentative start. It caused her to go short on her entry. It was not that bad; it was just enough, though, to reinjure her still fragile back. The physician helped her out of the pool and took her out of the competition. She would not be able to finish her last two dives. She was not seriously injured, but she would not be able to make the team. It was really sad.

There was another member of our diving team who used Mental Rehearsal extensively in preparing for the Olympic trials. This diver had started the practice of Mental Rehearsal much earlier, in a dance class when he was three years old. His enlightened teacher at the time had her students imagine their choreographed routines to music as they lay on the floor. He continued using this powerful yet practical technique throughout his dancing and diving careers. His name is Greg Louganis.

If you have not heard of him or seen him dive, just know that he was one of the best ever. He transformed the sport. He won four Olympic gold medals and several World Championships, and was the Outstanding Athlete of the 1988 Olympic Games. He profited even more than Pam from using Mental Rehearsal to maximize his potential.

After many years of practice with world-class athletes and performing artists, I reluctantly came to the conclusion that Mental Rehearsal really does work. When practiced correctly, it can be extremely effective in improving performance under pressure. I'm a convert; let me share what I've learned.

For the following Mental Rehearsal exercise, you'll need to set aside at least ten quiet, uninterrupted minutes alone. Pick a time when you'll be alert. If you do this practice when you're sleepy, you will probably drift off before you reach the happy ending. Then it will be about as useful as putting a textbook under your pillow.

You can practice Mental Rehearsal either sitting in a chair or lying down. Just make sure that your back is relatively straight and that you feel comfortable.

START WITH CENTERING Begin by forming a clear intention appropriate to this Mental Rehearsal. For example, your intent could be to imagine yourself doing your shifts in tune. Select your *visual reference point:* the physical location where you will imagine yourself beginning. It could be your music stand, for example.

Close your eyes. For at least a minute, focus only on breathing slowly and fully, in through your nose and out your mouth. Then do a total body scan; go from head to toe. Check your head and facial muscles, your jaw, neck, shoulders, arms, wrists, hands, rib cage, back, hips, thighs, calves, ankles, and feet. Release any tension that you find, until your muscles are deeply relaxed and you feel very comfortable, unfettered by body noise.

For the next minute, be mindful of only your Center. Then choose an appropriate Process Cue, just as you would in real life. To continue with our example, your Process Cue could be, "smooth shifts." Say your Process Cue to yourself until you're in your right brain, feeling, seeing, and hearing smooth shifts.

FOCUS ON YOUR VISUAL REFERENCE POINT This is your starting point. In our example, it's your music stand. See it in your mind's eye. At first, it may look fuzzy. That's normal; your mental clarity will improve with practice.

You can view the scene either from an inside or an outside perspective. You can imagine yourself looking around your practice room or you can be a voyeur, of sorts, watching yourself from somewhere else. Just do whatever's easier. Eventually, you'll want to alternate both inside and outside perspectives for a complete picture.

HAVE A MULTISENSORY EXPERIENCE Don't stop there. Make sure that you're also able to feel your hands on your instrument. If you're a singer, notice how your voice feels. Listen closely to the acoustics; pay attention to how you sound. This entire experience should seem as real and as vivid as possible.

IMAGINE WHAT YOU WOULD LIKE The primary goal here is to imagine yourself in Optimal Performance mode. Try to see, feel, and hear yourself performing well, but don't get upset if it's not perfect.

CORRECT YOUR MISTAKES Mental Rehearsal gives you a marvelous, effective way to correct mistakes. Mistakes are normal in Mental

Rehearsal, just as in life. If you imagine missing a shift, for example, hit the stop button on your mental VCR immediately. Rewind to a place before the mistake. Start from that point, moving slowly forward at a speed you can control. Repeat this process several times, just as you would in real practice, until you can perform it well in your mind in real time.

LAYER YOUR SEGMENTS Break up your material into ten-minute sections. The first session might begin with your warm-up in the green room, then going onstage and starting out well. The next session might pick it up from there and go into the middle of the second piece. The following one would continue from there to the end of the performance. Work up to the point where you can imagine yourself performing all three pieces back to back, finishing with thundering applause.

BE CREATIVE AND HAVE FUN

Expand your use of Mental Rehearsal. Take on new repertoire. Imagine yourself performing it in different locations under varying circumstances. Keep the sessions fun and interesting.

The more you hear those beautiful sounds, feel your smooth moves, and clearly envision how well you can do, the more your real-life performing will improve. Strive to practice Mental Rehearsal every day. Now it's time to apply the technique to your music. The following exercise has three parts.

First, perform one of your repertoire pieces and give yourself an overall rating from 1 to 100 in the box below.

Second, complete several Mental Rehearsals on that same selection of music. Remember, Mental Rehearsal sessions begin with Centering. Make sure that you mentally warm up. See the music on the stand, feel the instrument in your hands (or sense your vocal support), and hear your sound. Then start by going through the piece.

Keep in mind that when you make a mistake, you need to back up a few bars and correct it before going on. Initially, keep your sessions short (seven to ten minutes) and make them fun. Imagine yourself performing at the beach or in your favorite place.

Record your observations and insights in the Mental Rehearsal Log below. Note the clarity of what you see and the quality of what you hear and feel. The Process Goal for this drill is to be able to imagine yourself performing the piece correctly all the way though.

Finally, when you are ready, perform the piece again in real life and rate it below.

DATE: _____ PIECE: _____

RATING: _____

_____

Mental Rehearsal Log

DATE	LENGTH OF SESSION	CLARITY	QUALITY	CONTROL	COMMENTS

DATE: _____ PIECE: _____

RATING: _____

_____

EMOTIONAL APPROACH

How do you feel in the days, hours, and moments leading up to a critical and consequential performance? We'll refer to those feelings, whatever they may be, as your *Emotional Approach*. In this section, we'll explore your willingess to risk, your concerns about the possibility of failing and fears you may harbor to do with success.

	LOW							MID-RANGE								HIGH
The Ability to Risk	20 25 30 35 40 45 50 55 60 65 70 75 80 85 90 95 100															
	Cautious														Go For It
Risking Defeat	20 25 30 35 40 45 50 55 60 65 70 75 80 85 90 95 100															
	Tentative														Courageous
Risking Success	20 25 30 35 40 45 50 55 60 65 70 75 80 85 90 95 100															
	Fearful														Embrace Success

The Ability to Risk

The Ability to Risk category concerns your emotional intent leading up to your performance, especially when you feel you have the most to lose. High scores are found in courageous individuals who are willing to take necessary chances to perform their best. The higher your score, the more you are able to pull out the stops and *Go For It*.

A mid-range score in this category indicates that you sometimes take an unnecessarily cautious approach to upcoming events. You might say to yourself on the morning of an important performance or audition: "If they don't seem friendly, or if I feel uncomfortable, I will just play conservatively."

> *The biggest risk in life is not risking.*
>
> —ROBERT ANTHONY

Low scores point to a tentative or hesitant approach to performing. Hesitancy sets up poor beginnings, and no one is impressed with a wimpy start, least of all you and your well-fed internal critics. For performing artists, the ability to take appropriate risks is an essential skill. If you have a low score in the Ability to Risk, you will find the upcoming exercise on *Building Courage* to be helpful.

Risking Defeat

The Risking Defeat category measures your courage in facing the real possibility of failure in consequential performance situations. High scores go to performers who know how to deal effectively with this fear so that their performance is unaffected. They don't worry or engage in Doomsday Thinking. These performers tend to thrive and do well in high-pressure situations like auditions and critical performances.

If your score in this category is mid-range, you may experience a moderate level of fear and anxiety. You are neither totally preoccupied with, nor fully oblivious to, the possibility of failure. It may be that you are more courageous in some situations and more fearful in others.

> *There are risks and costs to a program of action. But they are far less than the long-range risks and costs of comfortable inaction.*
>
> —JOHN F. KENNEDY

A low score would indicate that you harbor a strong fear of failure. This fear often feeds on itself, driving anxiety and Activation levels through the roof. In the process, muscle tension, Doomsday Thinking, and Obsessing about Results often spiral. But take heart. You can learn how to handle this fear.

Risking Success

Not every outcome of success is experienced as positive. Hence the phrase, *fear of success*. You may feel guilty about knocking a friend out of a competition for a prize or position. This can be a painful conflict. Also, your own personal best performance can raise others' expectations, not to mention those of your internal scorekeepers.

Winning when you do not expect to win can bring on stress. You may have neglected to make child-care arrangements for the final round of an audition because you never expected to make it that far. You may have a comfortable tenured position in a B-level orchestra. Having made the semifinals for a major orchestra job, you may suddenly confront the upsetting

> *True success is overcoming the fear of being unsuccessful.*
>
> —PAUL SWEENEY

possibility of moving to a new city for the position. High scores are often found in performers with experience and confidence handling success and everything that comes with it.

A mid-range score in Risking Success indicates that you feel a moderate level of fear surrounding the possibility of realizing your potential. This may or may not have a hindering effect on your work. A low score in this category means that you genuinely fear success. You have probably found effective ways to limit your own potential.

> *We fear our highest possibility (as well as our lowest one). We are generally afraid to become that which we can glimpse in our most perfect moments.*
>
> —ABRAHAM MASLOW

Rationalizations abound: you may seek to avoid pain, stress, and potential embarrassment. Later in the book, you can learn how to embrace success.

For many performers, there is a Bigger Fear. The Bigger Fear is: "What if I really, really, tried my very hardest, and it still wasn't good enough? What would I do then? I couldn't deal with it. Deep down, it would confirm that I just don't have the goods. My house of cards would come crashing down. I would be devastated." That's the big one for many artists.

It's a shame that so many performers get stuck and allow this fear to preclude or delay the success that they would seem to be working so hard to achieve. The Bigger Fear can destroy dreams, or at least put them off until they just seem to fade away. There are strategies for dealing effectively with this fear. If you are willing to examine it in the light of your conscious awareness, you can start to learn how to get past it.

Building Courage

If I have learned anything through working with Olympic divers, race-car drivers and audition winners, it is that courage is the best choice in high-pressure situations. Unfortunately, we are socialized in this country to be afraid. Thanks mostly to movies, television, and newspapers, we carry around a lot of unnecessary fear. For performing artists, this general preoccupation with playing it safe can lead to tentativeness and hesitation, especially at the beginning of pieces.

Many performers back into their entrances. If the opening goes acceptably, they let go a bit more, and if that is okay, then they might let go some more. On instruments like the violin, where minute finger slips can result in huge disaster, this approach is understandable. But it's not Optimal. You need to be able to Go For It if you want to succeed at anything involving complex movement skills. Whether that is the physical move that accompanies a musical attack, moving air though your wind column, or driving a race-car, you need to Go For It even when all your instincts are screaming, "No!"

> *Courage is doing what you're afraid to do. There can be no courage unless you're scared.*
> —EDDIE RICKENBACKER

Leading up to important events, you need to commit that you are going to Go For It, *no matter what*. Then, when the time comes, you will be able to trust your talent and experience Going For It.

A few years ago, a prominent Manhattan voice teacher referred one of her students to me. This singer was nailing everything in her lessons, but she was terrified of auditions. She would go into every one and just bomb. Her teacher told her that if she was not able to get past her audition fears, there was no sense continuing with the voice lessons, no matter how well she was singing in them.

She completed her Artist's Performance Survey, and we discovered that she had a number of debilitating fears. In addition to her worries about auditions and failing, this woman had strong fears of many things. Fear was tying her up in knots, not just in her singing, but in every aspect of her life. She had a lot of talent and great practice habits and was vocally well trained. Her fears were preventing her from showing her abilities to anyone other

> *What happens to me, given any situation, I can handle it.*
> —SUSAN JEFFERS

than her friends or teacher. In spite of years of dedication and a huge financial investment, she had yet to win any professional roles or even an apprentice position.

I recommended that she read the book *Feel the Fear and Do It Anyway,* by Dr. Susan Jeffers (Fawcett Columbine, 1987). It's an excellent resource for any person facing the inevitable fear issues of performance.

I also gave the singer my Courage Exercise to complete. (You'll read about the Courage Exercise in a minute.)

A few months later, she called with two exciting announcements: she had won an audition for her first professional role in an off-Broadway show, an adaptation of *Carmen*. She was in the title role and she was very happy about that. The other thing she told me was that she had gone bungee-cord jumping. I was astounded. This was a woman who had been nearly paralyzed by fear. She had learned how to get past her fears by building her courage.

All living race-car drivers have learned one valuable lesson, if nothing else. It is known as *Trailing Throttle Oversteer* or *TTO*. It is one of the first lessons taught in race-car driving schools, and it is very important for apprentice drivers—and performing artists—to know how TTO works. It functions, by the way, just the same for passenger cars on highways as it does for Indy cars at the Miami Grand Prix. That's why there are guardrails on most highway off-ramps, to catch the results of this classic mistake by untrained drivers.

> *In times of stress,*
> *be bold and valiant.*
>
> —HORACE

Here is how it goes. You are driving a few minutes behind schedule on some superhighway, going too fast. You come to your exit.

You start into your turn and then you realize that you are going way too fast as you approach the OSP or *Oh Shit Point*. The instinctive, fearful move when you hit the OSP is to hit the brakes and clutch at whatever you happen to be holding at the time. If that is a steering wheel, or a musical instrument, your grip pressure will tighten (fig. 1).

Every motorist who hits the brakes at the OSP is going to set up a potentially dangerous situation. This is what it looks like (fig. 2).

If you are carrying too much speed as you start to make the turn on the off-ramp, you will start into the turn before hitting the brakes at the OSP. This will send the car's weight to the front of the vehicle, making the back end "light." Since a turn has been started, the light back end will tend to continue turning in the same direction and start spinning around (fig. 3).

In a race car, you don't need to hit the brakes for this occur. Merely lifting your foot off the accelerator, or "trailing off the throttle" after starting a turn will cause the vehicle to oversteer (and spin like a top). It is the one of the most dangerous things you can do in any car. For the unknowing motorist, it causes crashes into guardrails. For racers, it sets up broadside hits.

Experienced drivers don't allow the instinctive fear response to cause them to tense up and slow down. Rather than grab the wheel too tight and take their foot off the gas, they keep their upper body relaxed and accelerate through the turn. That's right; they step on the gas as they hit the OSP, when everything inside them is screaming to do just the opposite. If they follow the counsel of fear, they will lose. Maybe big-time. The safest and fastest way through the turn is the courageous choice.

The next time you are on a superhighway, notice the skid marks on the off-ramps and the dents on the guardrails made by motorists who allowed fear to dictate their instinctive response. In race-car driving schools, students hit the OSP at faster and faster speeds while they practice getting on the gas and accelerating through turns. It makes cars move like slingshots through turns. It is quite a thrill, and it's much better than spinning out.

Whether it is a race car, a double-reed instrument, or singing a high C sharp, they all require that you make the courageous choice to trust your talent and training and Go For It under extreme circumstances. The more you make that choice, the better it gets.

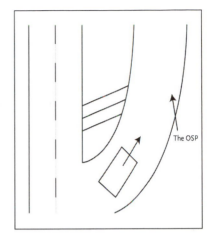

Fig. 1

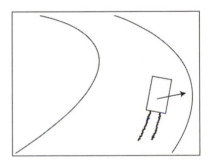

Fig. 2

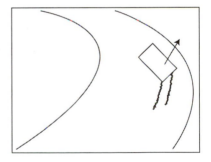

Fig. 3

Later in the book, you will develop your ability to Go For It, first in private, then under more pressured circumstances. You will reach the point where it's a done deal; you are going to Go For It, from the very first note, *no matter what.*

OVERCOMING FEARS OF SUCCESS

Many performing artists have trouble relating to the concept of *fear of success*. It's just not an issue for them. If you are fortunate in this way, I hope you continue to be so. Please feel free to skip past this section. On the other hand, perhaps you are one of those performers who do in fact experience a dread of success. You might worry that you will feel more pressure from heightened expectations. You may be uncomfortable about beating a friend in competition. Or perhaps you're concerned about what might happen if you really did perform your best when it counted.

> *Coraggio.*
>
> —MARIA CALLAS,
> *MASTER CLASS*

As long as you are unable to imagine yourself dealing effectively with whatever issues that may accompany your best, you will prevent yourself from experiencing success. The fear will limit you unless you know what to do.

In the box below, list ten past events when you did well but experienced difficulties as a result. Next to the event, write down what those specific problems were. In the next column, describe how you dealt with each of them.

SUCCESSFUL EVENT	PROBLEMS THAT RESULTED	HOW YOU DEALT WITH THEM

Now, in the next box, write out some of your current fears of success. Include all your worries and concerns about the potential pain, disappointment, or pressure that success might bring in the future. The process of writing these down will shine your conscious awareness on them. When you look at each one in the light, you start to handle them.

Go down the list, one at a time, writing out several options for dealing with each fear. Consider a variety of possible strategies and numerous contingency plans. Now those problems may not look so bad to you, after all.

FEAR	HOW YOU COULD DEAL WITH IT

GOING FOR IT

The way you approach important performances has everything to do with how those performances ultimately turn out. Building courage is a must. Optimal Performance requires that you Go For It, especially on first notes and passages. Tentativeness and easing into pieces does not work. It takes courage to Go For It under pressure.

For this exercise, get out the music for your three repertoire selections. On the music itself, mark the end of the opening phrase of each work. (A few bars is typical.) Then leave the room. Come back in as if you are walking onto a stage. Perform each of those opening sections one after the other, pausing only briefly between each. When you've done all three, rate your courage on a scale from 1 to 100, with 1 being a wimp and 100 being Rocky Balboa (remember him?). Next to each rating, feel free to make notes about your approach.

REPERTOIRE PIECE	RATING	COMMENTS

If your score was lower than you'd like, you need to repeat this exercise, understanding that you need to raise your commitment level. When you go out the door, think about your going for it. Do not come back in to perform until you have made a firm commitment that you will Go For It.

The Process Goal of this exercise is that you Go For It on all three pieces without hesitation. Once your score is 90 or above (at least up to the level of Indiana Jones), you can move on.

COMMITTING TO GO FOR IT		
REPERTOIRE PIECE	RATING	COMMENTS
_____	_____	_____
_____	_____	_____
_____	_____	_____
_____	_____	_____
_____	_____	_____
_____	_____	_____

ATTENTION

Complex as they are, none of the performing arts seem to compare in difficulty to the challenge of remaining focused in live performance. With all the potentially distracting things that can go on, it's amazing that there are not more mistakes. A violin virtuoso may stun listeners with a Paganini *Caprice* at top speed, yet be struggling throughout with left-brain thoughts and worries about what her critics will say. A pianist may bang out a Rachmaninoff concerto, all the while plagued by the sound of someone opening candy wrappers in the balcony.

	LOW					MID-RANGE									HIGH		
Object of Focus	20	25	30	35	40	45	50	55	60	65	70	75	80	85	90	95	100
	Others																The Process
Focusing Past Distractions	20	25	30	35	40	45	50	55	60	65	70	75	80	85	90	95	100
	Distracted																Unaffected
Mental Quiet	20	25	30	35	40	45	50	55	60	65	70	75	80	85	90	95	100
	Noisy																Quiet

The Object of Focus

This category indicates what you tend to focus on while performing, and your level of concern with what others' may think about your perform-ing. A high score means that you are process-oriented, focused from the in-side on what merits your attention. As you perform, you focus on your sound, without taking time or energy to worry what others—audience members, crit-ics, colleagues—may think of you or your music. This recommended ap-proach is known as *inside-out*.

> *Nothing interferes with my concentration. You could put an orgy in my office and I wouldn't look up. Well, maybe once.*
>
> —ISAAC ASIMOV

With a mid-range score in this cate-gory, you may be able to achieve this Optimal Performance state at times, but not often enough, and not necessar-ily as a conscious action. If you scored low in this category, you tend to be preoccupied with other people's opinion of your work. This other-directed attention is known as *outside-in* and is always a liability. Every performer should know how to perform from the inside out, focused on the Process to the exclusion of everyone else. More on this later.

Focusing Past Distractions

Anything can happen in live performance. Your music stand could fall over, the lights could go out, your E string could pop. A high score in Focusing Past Distractions means that you know how to direct your attention past external events of all kinds, *no matter what*. You're relatively unaffected by the sights or sounds of unexpected occurrences. You're able to remain focused on the process and task at hand. Bravo!

> *Concentration is everything.*
>
> —LUCIANO PAVAROTTI

A mid-range score in this category indicates that you have a less consist-ent response to startling outside occur-rences: sometimes you're able to keep your attention on the task at hand; at other times, not. Some things may bother you more than others. You may not mind the sight of latecomers arriving in the hall, for example, but a cell phone ringing could wipe you out, causing you to turn two pages at once. And now you're lost in the middle of a piece. Yikes.

A low score in Focusing Past Distractions means that you are very distractible by events happening around you. If so, are you thrown off by sights, or sounds, or both? You'll soon learn how to construct an *Attentional Boundary* between yourself and all such distractions.

Mental Quiet

Concentration is like a still pond. Each left-brain thought is a pebble that disrupts the peaceful right-brain state of Optimal Performance. A high score in Mental Quiet is found in performers who know how to achieve the right-brain state known as *Alpha*. They can then pay full attention to executing their complex skills and movement patterns without distracting internal noise. They understand that those skills will happen on their own, without left-brain interference

Optimal Performance and Peak Performance states are literally beyond words. They come from the quiet, Alpha mind-state, in which clear images, beautiful sounds, and wonderful feelings are allowed to flow. That's why you spend hours and hours to refine your technique and practice your material over and over and over again: so that you can experience the joy of letting it fly. You earned it.

If you have a low or even mid-range score, you need to learn to switch from your left brain to your right brain, as part of your *pre-event routine,* something you do each time before you start. We'll cover that later.

Mental Boundaries

There will always be potential distractions in life, regardless of what you're doing. As you watch television and pay attention to the images on the screen, you rarely notice the television itself. The figures on the screen capture your attention, so you concentrate on the show and totally disregard the television set itself.

You may at this point be relatively unaware of any background noise, such as the usual hum of the television, refrigerator, or ceiling fan. Once you become consciously aware of any of these background noises, however, they can take your attention away. For example, once you think the hum of the television needs a technician's attention, you're no longer focused on the dialogue, music, or images on the screen. You're off your task of watching television.

In performance, of course, the stakes are higher. As your attention focuses on something, you need to decide whether or not it is task-relevant. Ask yourself if it helps you in any way do what you need to do. Or is it task-irrelevant, having nothing to do with the job at hand? In performance, if a thing is task-irrelevant, simply do not attend to it. But don't try to block it out. The more you attempt to block it out, the more attention you give it, and the more distracting it becomes. Simply pay it no mind.

CONSTRUCTING YOUR BOUNDARY

Artists experience difficulty under pressure because their skills are complex and challenging. There is little room for error. In performance, you are judged not only on technique, but also on your ability to open up and reveal deeper and more sensitive aspects of yourself. When properly used, imaginary boundaries can give you a sense of protection in adverse circumstances.

Not everyone in such situations is nice or on your side. Audition panels, audiences, and other performers may do whatever they choose while you are performing. They may talk, shuffle papers, eat snacks, or just ignore you altogether while you pour yourself out, heart and soul (fig. 4). You don't want to let anything like that undermine your work. A boundary can shield you from anything that is task-irrelevant, while keeping your focus within your area of control.

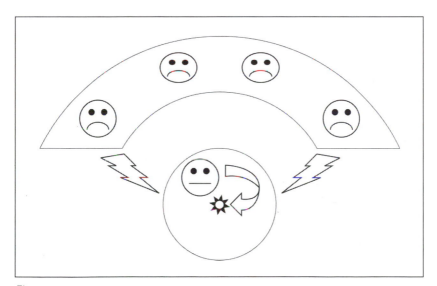

Fig. 4

I encourage you to create your own unique version of a personal boundary—one that will work for you. The boundary needs to encompass you, your instrument, and the area where you are to perform. It will allow your sound and image to go out, but nobody can cross it without your consent or interfere with your performance. You may start with an imaginary circle on the floor or think of a more spherical form that goes all around you (fig. 5).

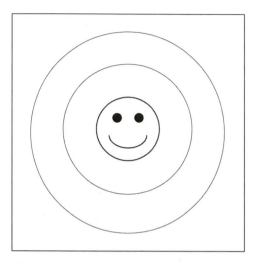

Fig. 5

One of the musicians at the Metropolitan Opera Orchestra uses a ring of fire as her boundary. An instrumentalist I know in Los Angeles surrounds himself with a group of lions, all facing out. One of my freelance clients uses a moat filled with alligators to give her a sense of security when she is performing.

You might choose a cylinder of steel, a cone of colored light, or a *Star Trek*–type force field surrounding you—whatever works (fig. 6). One singer in New York uses the image of a clear plastic eggshell all around her. Right before she goes onstage, she Centers, and then zips up the front of the egg. She feels protected; it also keeps her focused on the

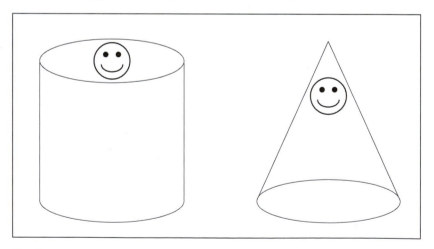

Fig. 6

immediate task at hand within the shell. It seems to work for her. She's won several auditions. Her name in my first book, *Audition Success*, was Veronica. Whatever your boundary, it will foster your sense of security and help you to focus better under extreme circumstances.

Whether it be a ring of fire, a cylinder of steel or a *Star Trek* force field, the idea is to make you feel protected from outside distractions. Any boundary you can imagine is worth testing out. The following exercise will help you determine which is the most effective for you.

First, assemble some sources of distraction. Try a radio set on a talk station, or possibly a TV tuned to an annoying infomercial, or maybe you could play a Yanni CD. If you find sweets irresistible, spread a table with cupcakes and candy. Just put together whatever distractions that will push your buttons.

Then play through all three repertoire pieces. If you find this easy, add more distractions—noise, movement or cupcakes—until you feel challenged to stay focused. The Process Goal of all this is to keep your focus within your boundary, No Matter What. Keep track of your progress and insights in the log on the following page. Repeat this exercise, changing or fortifying your boundary until you feel bullet-proof.

CONSTRUCT YOUR BOUNDARY

SOURCES OF DISTRACTION:

_____

_____

_____

_____

BOUNDARY:

_____

_____

_____

_____

COMMENTS:

_____

_____

_____

_____

Achieving Mental Quiet

Optimal Performance requires a state of mental quiet. Performing artists especially need to practice in the right-brain state of Alpha. It only takes a few minutes a day with this exercise.

First, put a relatively easy piece of music on the stand, and when you're ready, turn your tape recorder on.

Practice performing without all the left-brain noise. Do it on automatic pilot, using your Process Cue, kinesthetic abilities and muscle memory. When you can learn to do that on command, your ability to focus in performances will jump dramatically.

Keep track of your progress on the log below. After you are able to perform that piece in a state of predominantly right-brain quiet, gradually try it with more challenging works. The Process Goal is to be able to play each of your repertoire pieces in a state of mental quiet for at least 90% of the time.

ACHIEVING MENTAL QUIET		
PIECE OF MUSIC	LEFT-BRAIN NOISE	PROCESS CUE

Focusing Attention

Great artists captivate audiences with the sheer power of their *focus*. From the moment they begin to perform, they are totally absorbed in the moment. This deep immersion affords audience members a rare privilege. They can sit back, relax, and allow themselves to be pulled into a special world of intense focus.

You'll be impressed by how much difference improved concentration will make to your work. Not only will it help you sustain the attention that you need as a performer, but it will also enlarge and expand your magnetism as an artist.

Focus is essentially a right-brain, Alpha state of *mental quiet*. It's relatively free from distracting left-brain words. There are several different types of focus; they are best understood as a series of concentric circles (fig. 7).

> *A full mind is an empty baseball bat.*
>
> —BRANCH RICKEY

Awareness is the outer circle. It is the knowledge of what is happening around you and inside you. It may include the subtle sounds of the hall, nuances in your voice or instrument, or the passing sensations in your body. Awareness is the first aspect of concentration.

When you focus your awareness, you begin to pay *attention*. Right now, focus your awareness on the sounds in your surroundings. Stop for a moment and listen to something that a few seconds ago you did not hear, even though you may have been aware of it at a less-conscious level. An example would be the electrical hum of your refrigerator, your overhead light, or a computer that's on in your room.

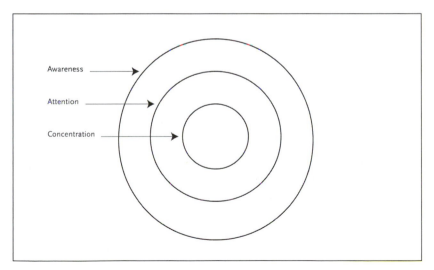

Fig. 7

As you start paying attention to this sound, you may note that it seems to increase in volume. Now you really hear it. You knew that it was there all the time, but you were not listening to it, since you were not selecting to attend to it. It was inconsequential and not worth noticing. The more you focus your attention on the sound, the "louder" it will get.

This is the *Gestalt* concept of *figure* versus *ground*. The more you focus your attention on a selected feature in your environment, or ground, the more you concentrate on that feature and disregard the background. This feature, or figure, becomes more prominent as you pay attention to it. Intent on such a figure as a television show, you rarely notice the ground, which would be the television set itself. The more you focus on the show, the more you disregard the TV set and all other potential distractions around you.

Moving closer to the center of our concentric circles, attention is the second ring. Attention is focused awareness. It refers to what you select to attend to and how you do so. There are two dimensions of attention: the *scope of attention* and the *direction of attention*.

The scope of attention goes from broad to narrow. You can have a wide focus or narrow it to a precise point. The direction of attention goes from external to internal (fig. 8). In other words, you can direct your focus on something outside yourself or on something inside yourself.

If you look at the point where the two lines intersect, you will have narrowed your scope of attention. Now leave your eyes there, but notice the entire page. Do it without moving your eyes. If you are aware of the

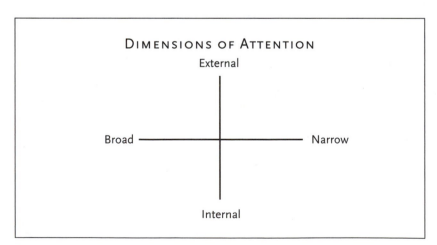

Fig. 8

full page, while letting your eyes settle at the intersection, your scope of attention is broad.

Now focus on only the point again. Then notice the page, then the entire room without moving your eyes from the intersection. That is the shift from a narrow to a broad scope of attention. It's not a movement or tracking of the eyes, but an attentional shift within the eye itself. We are constantly shifting our scope of attention from narrow to broad, and vice versa.

We're also constantly shifting our direction of attention from external to internal. As you focus your eyes on the intersection, and really see that point, you're directing your attention on external reality, on something outside of you. When you focus on other people, events or things outside of yourself, you're directing your attention externally. As long as you actually see the point on the page, you have an external focus of attention.

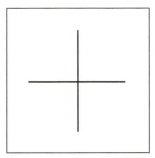

Fig. 9

As you let your eyes settle at the point, picture the front door of your house or apartment. Imagine what the doorknob looks like. If you are not able to see it immediately with your eyes open, take a second and close your eyes. Let the images come to you.

Now, while noticing the entire page, without focusing on any part, picture a good friend's face. Hear the sound of one of your favorite songs. Then notice what your left ankle feels like if you wiggle it around; scan your entire body to see where you may be holding tension. This is internally directed attention.

Then bring your attention from internal to external. See the period at the end of this sentence. That is the shifting of the direction of attention, from internal to external. It has little to do with whether your eyes are open, with a "soft" focus, or closed. As with the scope of attention, the direction of attention shifts back and forth.

This leads us to four types of attention:

Broad external attention, as when you noticed the entire room, is useful for navigating through complex environments such as concert halls and backstage areas. It can be a distraction if you need to be more narrowly focused, such as in Mental Rehearsal.

Narrow external attention, as when you focused on the intersection point and really saw it, is helpful for focusing on specific external targets.

Watching a conductor's subdivision of beats, for example, calls for this type of attention. But it can be a source of distraction if you need to be more aware of internal states, such as muscle tension.

Narrow internal attention, as when you pictured the doorknob or feel a pain in your knee, can be of immense value when checking key muscles for tension or focusing on certain outcomes. It's not helpful to be internally preoccupied, though, at critical moments in live performances when you need to be more externally aware of task-relevant things going on around you.

Broad internal attention, as when you scanned your body for tension, is also helpful for Mental Rehearsal. When you need to be paying attention to certain external events in reality, like the music, your script, or other performers, it can cause problems.

Flexibility of attention is critical because many of the shifts between the different types of attention need to occur in milliseconds or less, and often without conscious awareness. Important attentional shifts should be consciously planned out and rehearsed in advance to preclude otherwise-likely mistakes.

Optimal Performance requires that you use the appropriate types of attention for the demands of changing circumstances. Spy on great performers and you'll notice how smoothly and flexibly they switch between different types of attention. You can learn to do it too (fig. 10).

First, put one piece of music on the stand. Second, complete the box below, filling in the types of attention you plan to use in a Mock Performance of this piece.

Then go outside the room and warm up. Pause briefly outside the door, walk in the room, and perform the piece.

Finally, write your comments in the box on the following page. Your Process Goal is to use the appropriate type of attention at each point, from warming up to walking offstage. Repeat this exercise until you are consciously switching attention types smoothly and flexibly.

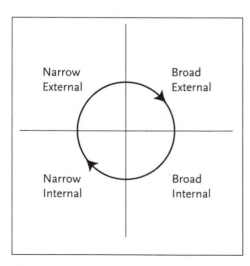

Narrow
External

Broad
External

Narrow
Internal

Broad
Internal

Fig. 10

```
┌─────────────────────────────────────────────────────────────┐
│                    ATTENTIONAL PLAN                         │
│                                                             │
│   CIRCUMSTANCE      TYPE OF ATTENTION      COMMENTS         │
│   Warming up        _____       │
│   Outside the door  _____       │
│   Walking in        _____       │
│   Checking music    _____       │
│   Tuning (if applicable)  _____       │
│   Right before first note  _____       │
│   The first note    _____       │
│   Between pieces    _____       │
│   During the third piece  _____       │
│   Walking offstage  _____       │
└─────────────────────────────────────────────────────────────┘
```

CONCENTRATION

Concentration often makes the difference between an Optimal, or even Peak Performance, and your everyday ho-hum stuff. The ability to focus is an absolute necessity for performing artists interested in performing their best. Concentration involves three parts: *Intensity, Presence,* and *Duration of Focus.*

	LOW	MID-RANGE	HIGH
Intensity of Focus	20 25 30 35 40 45 50 55 60 65 70 75 80 85 90 95 100 Weak		Powerful
Presence of Focus	20 25 30 35 40 45 50 55 60 65 70 75 80 85 90 95 100 Other Time or Place		Here and Now
Duration of Focus	20 25 30 35 40 45 50 55 60 65 70 75 80 85 90 95 100 Short		Until Done

Intensity of Focus

If anything gets to the heart of pure Concentration, it is Intensity of Focus. If you have a high score in this category, you can focus your attention to a powerful extent.

A mid-range score would indicate that you may be able to concentrate in some situations and not others. Or, the intensity of your Concentration depends on other variables, such as your preparation and rest.

If you have a low score in this category, you are not alone. The information coming up on Concentration and the related exercises will surely help you improve your Intensity of Focus.

Presence of Focus

The Presence of Focus category measures your ability to keep your attention in the here and now. Those with high scores concentrate on the task at hand. They do not dwell on the note they just missed or worry about the fast lick or high note coming up a few bars ahead, or, for that matter, anything else. They stay in the present, focused on the job.

A mid-range score shows that certain things affect your Concentration more than others. What yanks you out of the here and now? Do you tend to go back to mistakes or fret about upcoming difficulties? Or does your mind drift to unrelated events or other places? It's important to reflect on this.

A low score in Presence of Focus indicates that you do not focus very well. You might think: "Once again, Fred missed his entrance," Or "Oh God, the next movement's in 5/4 time," or "Will the conductor remember to cue me?" If so, you need to learn to keep your mind in the present and on your job. For help with that, the Centering process is indispensable.

Duration of Focus

The Duration of Focus score measures how long you sustain your concentration. A high score suggests that you are able to maintain your focus for as long as necessary. You win the big prize if you can hang in there through Mahler's Symphony No. 2 in E flat, which the *Guinness Book of Records* reports as the longest symphonic piece ever written.

A mid-range score in this category could mean either that you have a moderate attention span or that the length of your focus is dependent on circumstances and the amount of mental energy you have to expend.

A low score in Duration of Focus suggests that you have difficulty staying focused for any length of time. You need to learn how to maintain your Concentration for longer and longer periods of time.

Improving Your Concentration

As you have seen, Concentration involves three aspects: Presence of Focus, Intensity of Focus, and Duration of Focus. Performers need to concentrate in the here and now, intensely at times, until their perform-ance is over. Concentration requires your complete interest on a selected object to the exclusion of all else. This is total mindfulness, a fascination with the solitary chosen object, like a lover beholding his or her beloved.

Performers can get fully absorbed in a cocoon of Concentration, caught up in only what they are doing in the moment. Ideally, there is nothing else going on in the world for them other than the activity they're engaged in performing. If they're fortunate, that may be true for them for longer and longer periods.

Increasing Your Presence

While you're performing, if you think ahead to a tough part coming up or back to something you missed earlier, you will not be focused in the moment. Whenever your mind leaves the present, it causes breaks in your focus. Concentration is a temporary state at best; keeping your mind on one thing for any length of time is a challenge. It's normal for performers to "drift" in and out of focus, but it's not helpful.

The attention span of most children is from zero to four seconds; the attention span of most adults is four to seven seconds. Asian masters of concentration say that if you can focus exclusively on one thing for twelve sec-onds, you are a master. Try it. Choose whatever thing you would like, but focus on only that.

Imagine baby-sitting an active tod-dler, and trying to get her to stay within a three-foot circle for more than a few seconds. The child will stand still for only a moment before leaving to pursue something of interest. After the child is out of the circle, if you yell and find fault with her for not staying in the circle, she will run in any direction other than towards the circle.

> *When walking, walk.*
> *When eating, eat.*
> —ZEN MAXIM

When you are performing, if you are thinking about what someone else may be thinking, you are outside the circle. If you are worried about making a mistake or thinking about the ultimate results of your perform-ance or about what you might do afterwards, you are outside your circle. If you then find fault with yourself for not concentrating, you're making matters worse. You're moving farther away from being focused. The idea is to gently guide your attention, like you would the child, back on point.

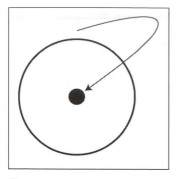

Fig. 11

You need to get back inside the circle, which represents your process, as soon as possible (fig. 11). Do not waste valuable time and energy criticizing yourself; just get back to the here and now as soon as possible. You can learn to do this faster and better; all it takes is practice and energy. Here's the drill.

Put the shortest piece of music on your stand. Whenever you're ready, perform the entire piece to the best of your ability. Your Process Goal is to keep your focus in the continuing and ever-changing here and now for at least 90 percent of the time.

In the Presence of Focus Log as shown below, write the name and length of the piece. Then rate your ability to remain focused on a scale from 1 to 100, with 1 being somewhere else in another space and time, and 100 being focused for the entire piece. Make notes on your progress. Be patient; this is not as easy as it appears at first glance. When you are able to perform all three pieces back to back in the here and now more than 90 percent of the time, you are ready to move on.

PRESENCE OF FOCUS LOG

PIECE OF MUSIC: _____ LENGTH: _____

DATE	CONCENTRATION RATING	OBSERVATIONS

Sustaining Your Intensity

It takes energy just to pay attention. You are less alert when tired and better able to focus when you are fresh and rested. Concentration takes an enormous amount of energy; it is not a passive state.

This precious and powerful energy needs to flow continually from your Center to appropriate points of focus. It is important to pace your expenditure of this resource. You need not only to focus at the beginning but also to maintain your Concentration throughout your entire piece or performance. This could be a minute or two or, in the case of Wagner, many hours. The longer the demands of the situation, the greater the need to pace the outflow of your energy.

Over the course of extended performances, it is crucial to expend your energy wisely. Expecting to maintain a Peak focus for an entire performance, from beginning to end, is neither reasonable nor practical. It will quickly deplete your Concentration energy. If you squander this vital resource too early in the program, it will not be available at the end, when it is often most needed.

> *To be able to concentrate for a considerable time is essential to difficult achievement.*
>
> —BERTRAND RUSSELL

If we plot that ill-advised approach, it would look like the diagram above (fig. 12). Concentration is on the vertical axis. It goes from low to high, from distracted to focused. Time is on the horizontal axis, from left to right.

It's not necessary to concentrate at an intense level at all times in most extended performances. You may find it helpful to plan out peaks, plateaus, and valleys for your focus. In every ensemble piece, and even in demanding solos of any length, there are times to fully concentrate, and times to relax focus and recover before focusing again. In that way,

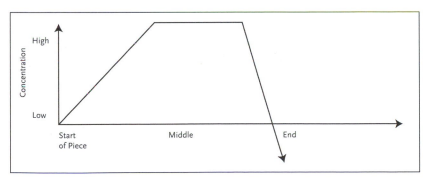

Fig. 12

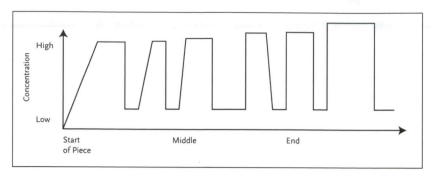

Fig. 13

Concentration can be sustained over long periods of time. That's how to achieve a superior performance in *The Ring Cycle* (fig. 13).

This does not mean that you should fall asleep in the middle of a performance. You simply maintain your awareness at a lower level of energy consumption whenever circumstances allow you to take momentary breaks. Then you can take brief respites to rest and recover some energy before you need to focus intensely again on worthy targets.

Achieving Singular Focus

The last aspect of focus is known as *One-Pointed Concentration*. This is a highly focused state, one of mystical unity. With this most central point of focus, there is a merging of subject and target. The archer and the

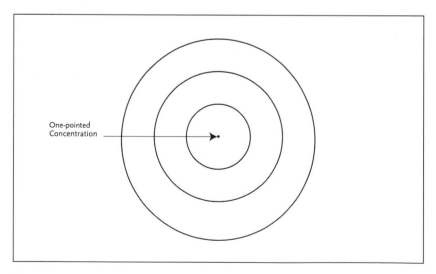

Fig. 14

84

bull's-eye become one. I know it sounds far out. It's way beyond the usual left-brain way of thinking.

With proper practice and dedication, though, one can achieve One-Pointed Concentration prior to and even during special performance moments. You cannot afford to spend an entire performance in that state. The changing demands of different performance situations require all types of focus, including relaxed awareness, proper Attention and good old Concentration. They all take energy, and your tank can only hold so much.

If you'd like to learn more about Concentration, I recommend *Zen in the Art of Archery*. The author, Eugen Herrigel, was a German professor who taught at the University of Tokyo and trained with a Zen master for six years. He thus brings a Western understanding to Eastern philosophy and its principles of Concentration. Though these archers close their eyes and turn their heads before releasing their arrows, they never miss.

One day the master cried out the moment my shot was loosed: "It is there!" Later, when I glanced towards the target . . . I saw that the arrow had only grazed the edge. "That was a right shot," said the master decisively, "and so it must begin. But enough for today, otherwise you will take special pains with the next shot and spoil the good beginning." (Eugen Herrigel)

RESILIENCE

The performing-arts world may not involve actual flying bullets or other physical danger, but the risks are real and the circumstances can be hostile. In your business, Resilience is essential. Whiners don't survive.

Let's think of Resilience as having three parts: your ability to let things happen under pressure rather than trying to force them, your response patterns to adverse circumstances, and the length of time you take to recover from unfortunate events.

Ease Under Pressure

Top performers are able to execute their craft with effortless power. High scores in Ease under Pressure are found in masterful artists who trust their talent and training and are able just to *Let It Go*, even under extreme circumstances.

	LOW								MID-RANGE							HIGH
Ease under Pressure	20	25	30	35	40	45	50	55	60	65	70	75	80	85	90	95	100
	Try Too Hard															Let It Go
The Ability to Fight	20	25	30	35	40	45	50	55	60	65	70	75	80	85	90	95	100
	Victim															Fighter
The Ability to Recover	20	25	30	35	40	45	50	55	60	65	70	75	80	85	90	95	100
	Delayed															Immediate

A mid-range score suggests that sometimes you try too hard. It could also mean that you have a conditional approach with your effort—sometimes you use more force than needed and at other times you allow things simply to happen. You'll benefit from experiencing the relationship between less effort and more power in the chapter on advanced training.

A low score in Ease under Pressure indicates a tendency to force things rather than just allowing them to occur. The lower your score, the greater your inclination to overeffort, especially when things are not going well. Your approach, when trying to get the round peg into the square hole, is to bring out the bigger hammer. Unfortunately, this compounds problems.

The Ability to Fight

This category reflects individual response patterns to adversity. High scores are found in performers who respond to tough circumstances as fighters. They often consider challenges as opportunities to practice overcoming obstacles. These individuals realize that performing well under pressure is often a battle. They're used to fighting and winning.

A mid-range score in the Ability to Fight category reveals that you have a more conditional response to inevitable performance difficulties. Sometimes you fight your way out of problems and at other times you act more like a helpless victim. It just depends.

A low score indicates a victim mentality, in which unfortunate things just seem to happen to you. You may feel hopeless, sorry for yourself, and powerless over unwanted circumstances. But you don't have to be a victim, and your performances need not suffer anymore. Stay tuned.

The Ability to Recover

In the performing arts, mistakes are part of the territory. If you don't believe me, ask Dale Clevenger. He recently told me that since becoming principal horn in the Chicago Symphony in 1966, he has never once played perfectly. Mistakes are going to happen. The idea is not to let them take you out of the present and cause additional problems. The longer you take to get over a lapse, the worse it gets.

The Ability to Recover score is a measure of how long it takes you to get back on track after making a mistake. High scores are noted in performers who are able to regain their focus and poise immediately after a mistake. A

> *Inside the ring or out, ain't nothing wrong with going down. It's staying down that's wrong.*
>
> —MUHAMMAD ALI

mid-range score suggests a less reliable response to external circumstances. Sometimes you respond quickly and at other times you bounce back after too long a delay. Such delays can be very costly. They keep you distracted, out of the present, and away from the task at hand. Other mistakes will follow.

A low score in this category indicates that you tend to get caught up in mistakes. There are many ways to delay your recovery from mistakes: perfectionism, denial, criticism, and Doomsday Thinking, not to mention left-brain analyses. All that noise, of course, just takes more time and brings on additional heartache. You'll soon examine what you do after mistakes and learn a strategy that will help you recover more quickly.

Training for the Fight

For all the dismay I feel about war and violence, I have the military to thank for one very profound lesson: deep within each of us is a fighter. My commando experience brought mine out. In a kinder way, I will strive to do the same for you.

This may strike you as a radical idea. As a musician, after all, you are a literal purveyor of harmony in this world. But the reality is that even in music—especially in music—you must confront battles on a daily basis. These may not involve tanks or artillery pieces, but they are battles just the same. I am talking about the battles you fight within yourself.

Several years ago, I was contacted by a soprano who was about to cancel her contract for the lead in Bernstein's *Candide*. The reason was due to her fear of one aria, "Glitter and Be Gay." She had a celebrated international career, but this one number was now scaring her away from a role she really wanted.

She and her husband had an adorable young son. After she told me about all the extremely challenging situations she had been through in her life, not to mention childbirth, I could not understand how she could be so intimidated by a song.

Then she sent me a recording of "Glitter and Be Gay." I soon realized what she was facing; no wonder she was scared. The song amounts to six minutes and forty-eight seconds of slugging it out with long, high runs. I couldn't fathom how anyone could pull it off at all, let alone in front of full houses, respected colleagues, and critics.

She said that she loved the challenge of doing well when circumstances were tough. She often found performing in extreme situations to be exciting and had grown to enjoy the experience. She liked seeing that she could do it regardless of external conditions. The more we explored those situations, the more evidence we found that she was a great fighter and a miserable victim. When she responded like a fighter, she was unstoppable. She enjoyed taking risks and she loved to perform. When she came out swinging, ready for her next challenge, she was truly awesome. She had the glowing reviews to prove it.

On the other hand, she could be a victim. When her internal, fear-of-failure voices convinced her that the situation was bigger than she was, she took on a passive role. She became near-helpless, feeling unable to do anything about the unfortunate circumstances. She hated her victim side, with good reason. Her mixed career results reflected that she had responded to some performance situations as a victim and to others as a fighter.

I taught her how to Center and encouraged her to practice it several times a day. Her Process Cues were to "Go For It" and "Fight." I recommended that she start working out, to get in better aerobic shape. She was to get in touch with her fighter by writing about the times that she had overcome adversity and done well. Her training regimen included the *Rocky* films and even using her anger as an additional source of energy when she chose to confront "Glitter and Be Gay."

On those occasions, she was to set it up correctly. Namely, she was to turn a tape recorder on in the room where she was going to Go For It. Then she was to leave the room, get her heart rate up, and imagine putting boxing gloves on. Then she was to come into the room, direct the energy right at the aria, and kick butt! The more she did that, the more she got on top of it. She was remembering what a great fighter she was, and she proved it to herself each time she did the drill.

The next part of her training was based on the sports psychology principle of overcompensation, namely, overdoing the required skill. After she got into the habit of nailing it every time, I encouraged her to sing the aria twice through without stopping. She was not so sure about the idea. The next time we spoke, though, she told me that she had sung it back to back and it went really well. After that, it would never be the same for her.

At one of the rehearsals, where she could have chosen to "mark" and not sing out, she chose to sing it and nailed it. The conductor was not pleased with the orchestra, so he indicated that he wanted to do it all over from the top, but that he didn't expect her to sing it again. She smiled and nailed it again. Awesome! Needless to say, it just got better after that. She told me later that her performance on opening night was one of the high points of her career.

So when you're ready, put your guard up and keep it up. Protect yourself at all times; it's a fight. I did not design the system; I just know what works well. Fighters tend to win, victims tend to lose. If you'd like to be more of a fighter, I suggest that you start looking for opportunities to confront adversity consciously with a purpose. It's a very important mind-set to develop. You have to be willing to go in there and use everything you have, then practice doing so under increasingly challenging circumstances against bigger obstacles.

Recovery Strategy

In my view, there are two critical situations that successful musicians handle exceptionally well: the first moments of performances, and the moments right after mistakes. The two situations call for completely different strategies.

Whereas you have days, months, and in some cases years to prepare for first notes, mistakes are by definition unplanned. It's what you do after they occur that matters most.

Before discussing damage-control strategies, let us recognize the importance that mistakes play in your development and mastery. Mistakes tell you that you are not doing something correctly. In so doing, they often outline the lower level of your skills and point up toward better ways.

Mistakes can also serve to outline the peak of your abilities. Those higher realms are worth exploring. Until you cross the upper line, you do not know how much room you have above your current tendencies.

Mistakes are thus a helpful consequence of "pushing the envelope," of pursuing your Optimal by taking certain risks. They can provide valuable feedback, letting you know where the edge is.

> *You're only human,*
> *you're supposed*
> *to make mistakes.*
>
> —BILLY JOEL

If every note in every piece is perfect, you may not be challenging your true talent and higher abilities enough. Tennis players who get every first serve in are not "playing the edge" of their capabilities. Until they start faulting, they don't know how much range they have for faster serves. Our faults and mistakes provide guideposts to our higher capabilities.

Those higher levels are worth pursuing—much more than perfection. If you are doing it correctly, performing in a state of high positive energy with a commitment to Go For It, you will make occasional mistakes. Such mistakes are not only okay but are recommended. They will let you know when you've pushed it just a bit too far. After such a mistake, you can cut back a little and know that you are close to the top.

Given the complexity of performing-arts skills executed in very stressful circumstances, mistakes are not only normal, but inevitable. Give yourself permission to miss a note now and then. The less you try to avoid mistakes at all costs, and the less horrible you make them, the more you will take them in stride. Occasional mistakes are okay. It's only when mistakes bring on subsequent mistakes that things become not okay.

What happens to you after you make a mistake? If you have a low score in Ability to Recover, you probably get too caught up in the mistake and delay your recovery. The more you understand what usually occurs after you make a mistake, the more immediate the solution can be.

What responses and thoughts are delaying you, after a mistake, from being focused on the task at hand? Where do you tend to tighten as part of the "cringe" response to a serious error? Does your mind go into left-brain analyses? Do your negative critics start screaming?

After you clearly understand what your usual response pattern is to mistakes, and realize that the left brain takes precious time to go through its distracting litany, you will be in a position to make better choices. Awareness is the key. The goal is not to try to eliminate mistakes altogether, but to get back on track quickly and efficiently after individual mistakes occur.

You need to have an emergency procedure and practice it in a safe environment before testing it in the heat of battle. This procedure needs to stop the bleeding and limit the damage. Assuming that you may make a mistake at some point in your career, you'll need to have a plan.

Following mistakes, many performers go into a time-consuming pattern of denial. It may sound something like: "I *can't believe* I came in wrong; I always count my rests correctly," or "I can't be out of tune, I just put on new strings yesterday." Whatever form your denial takes, and wherever the real blame lies, keep in mind that the beat goes on.

1) ACCEPT THE MISTAKE

You need to accept reality as soon as possible. This does not mean that you have to do so with a happy face. You may be very angry, but for the moment your feelings just aren't relevant. You'll have plenty of time for that later. You've made one mistake; don't make it worse.

2) GET BACK INTO THE PRESENT

Letting your mind drift back to what may have caused the mistake and taking time to assess the damage or worry about similar passages later in the piece will diminish your focus. Following a mistake, it is important that you bring your mind back into the present without any delay.

3) RELAX YOUR KEY MUSCLES

Mistakes frequently cause muscles to tighten. Rather than deny a mistake, let it serve as a cue to remind you to release excess tension. This is especially true if you're feeling angry. You need to insure that your body is free and supple. In the heat of battle, this is much more functional than denying or analyzing your mistake. Releasing tension in your key muscles will help.

4) SAY YOUR EMERGENCY PROCESS CUE

Create a Process Cue specifically for emergency use. It will help you get back into your right brain, focused on the relevant task at hand. You might choose something like: "Stay with it," or "Keep it rolling." Have your emergency Process Cue in mind before you start any performance. Like a fire extinguisher, have it handy; you never know when you're going to need it.

5) PERFORM AT A REASONABLE LEVEL

This may seem obvious, but I have seen too many elite performers try to make up for mishaps by attempting to pull off some incredible feats directly afterward. This tends to compound the problem. Trying to make up for bad notes with great notes only causes more bad notes.

The idea is damage control, pure and simple. Just stop the bleeding. This is not the time to try to pull off something spectacular. That will just make matters worse; you will dig yourself into a deeper hole. If you are recovering from Suboptimal levels, you will need to focus on the process of doing "pretty well" before you play around with Peak Performance. Lay a solid foundation for Optimal Performance first. Be reasonable.

Remember, audition panels and paying audiences are not looking for perfection; they want to feel the excitement of someone hanging it out on the edge. That's risky. If a mistake happens because of that, though, and you are able to recover immediately and effortlessly, you may earn more than their respect.

This is the 5-step recovery strategy I recommend. Now you'll have an opportunity to put it into practice. Here's how it works.

First, get out your most challenging piece and put it on the stand. When you are ready, play it until you make a mistake. If you get through the piece without making a mistake, play it again until you do. If necessary, choose another piece.

When you make a mistake, don't stop. Rather, continue past the mistake for at least one minute. Then stop. In the box below, write out the sequence of events, thoughts, and feelings that you experienced following the mistake. How did these affect your performance after the mistake? For example, having chipped a high note, you may cringe, tighten your shoulders, and feel embarrassed. You may go on to deny that you could ever have missed that note. As these activities occupy your attention, you miss the next entrance altogether. Oops! *&ˆ@%#!

Your Process Goal is to let mistakes be isolated events. Do this exercise until you are able to recover from mistakes quickly and without incident.

BECOMING RESILIENT

What are your initial responses after you make a mistake?

_____

Where do you tend to tighten up?

_____

What feelings do you experience?

_____

What are your usual thoughts?

_____

What happens to your attention?

_____

How can you improve your speed of recovery?

_____

_____

_____

Comments:

_____

_____

_____

_____

_____

5.

Advanced Training

Put Your New Skills to Work

MAKE A SECOND TAPE

I T'S TIME AGAIN to take stock of your performance abilities by making a tape, just as you did at the beginning of this book. Again, choose three contrasting excerpts or solos to perform. (You can do the same repertoire you used before.) Start with a relatively easy selection, move on to a mid-level one, and finish with something very challenging. The total length of the selections performed back to back should be from fifteen to thirty minutes.

Set everything up ahead of time. Make sure that your performance space is ready and that your equipment is in order. You can invite some colleagues or acquaintances, even family members, to the session. Or just do it on your own with your friendly recording device.

Take as long as you would like before you begin the performance, but once the tape is rolling, keep going. Do not stop until you reach the end, no matter what happens. You may pause briefly—no more than twenty seconds—between selections.

Immediately after you've completed all three works, make a few comments on the tape about how you performed. Give each piece a subjective rating on a scale from 1 to 100, with 1 being your worst nightmare and 100 being You Got the Job. Also cite examples of what you did well and what could have been better. Then and only then turn the recorder off.

TAPING #2

DATE: _____ TIME: _____ LOCATION: _____

Part/Piece Excerpt	*Rating*	*Strengths*	*Areas to Improve*
_____	_____	_____	_____
_____	_____	_____	_____
_____	_____	_____	_____

EVALUATOR'S NAME: _____ DATE: _____

Part/Piece Excerpt	*Rating*	*Comments*
_____	_____	_____
_____	_____	_____
_____	_____	_____

If you had a colleague or teacher present, have him or her also rate and comment on your performance. If you did not have such a person present at the recording session, give him or her the tape soon afterward. Write down the score he or she gives you as well as his or her comments. Don't forget to label the tape with your name and the date.

SET YOUR GOALS

Based on the tape you just made, what are the technical and musical points that you need to work on most? Pick one of those right now. Improving in this area will be your one-month Outcome Goal. Make sure it's reasonable yet challenging. Say, for example, that you were pleased with certain aspects of your performance, but regret that you missed four of the ten high notes. A good Outcome Goal for you would be to perform all the pieces hitting eight or more of the high notes.

> *Everything's in my mind. That's where it all starts. Knowing what you want is the first step toward getting it.*
>
> —MAE WEST

One-Month Outcome Goal: _____

So how are you going to achieve that goal? The first thing you must do is reflect on the causes of the performance flaw or flaws in question. In our example, you may realize that you engaged in Doomsday Thinking about some of those high notes.

Origins of Performance Problem: _____

What are the specific techniques you can apply? One way to address Doomsday Thinking, for example, is through Mental Rehearsal. Figure out what would work best for you.

Applicable Technique: _____

Whatever you choose to work on, set your progress with the technique as a one-month Process Goal. To stay with our example, your Process Goal would be able to Mentally Rehearse that section of the music in real time without mistakes. When you feel you have succeeded with that goal, be sure to reward yourself.

One-Month Process Goal: _____

Reward: _____

You're almost there. Now you need to plan the applicable technique into your daily practice schedule. For example, if you plan on using Mental Rehearsal to help you hit eight or more of the high notes, you should practice Mental Rehearsal seven to fifteen minutes a day, four or five days a week, for the next four weeks. That's a lot. That's why you set rewards ahead of time.

Practice Structure: _____

_____

SIMULATION TRAINING

Warning: The drills in this section are intended to mimic some of the symptoms of high stress and prepare you to perform in an Optimal state. They require that you raise your pulse well above your resting heart rate. If you have a history of any medical condition or are currently being treated by any health professional, or are presently taking any medication, please get your physician's approval prior to doing this drill.

In preparation for an important performance, it's not enough to practice your repertoire until you're able to play it marvelously well. You can practice your music until you're blue in the face, but that just won't cut it. You've got to evoke in yourself the symptoms you will feel in actual performance, and do well in spite of them. And guess what? Even that is not enough. I want you to be able to thrive under truly extreme conditions. That's why so many of my clients win auditions. After they go through the simulation and adversity training you are about to do, a symphony audition is, relatively speaking, a walk in the park.

Turn back to page 35 to look at the highest point of your Optimal Activation range. This is your starting point. To simulate worse-than-real-life conditions, you will need to get your Activation way above that point.

Set up your practice room so there is a clear path from the door to the spot where you will perform. If you play an instrument, tune it ahead of time and put it in a convenient and accessible place. If you need time to warm up, please take it. Put your easiest repertoire piece on the music stand. Turn your tape recorder on and leave the room.

Now get your Activation up. You can do this any way you like. You could run up a flight of stairs, you could do jumping jacks, you could run in place. The goal is to get your heart going faster than it ever would in a performance situation. This shouldn't take more than a minute or two. You want to get to the point where you feel your heart pounding—but if you are sweaty or breathless, you are overdoing it.

After you have your heart rate up, pause' outside the room and quickly Center Down. Open the door and go in. Right before you start, notice your Activation level.

After you begin, keep going, no matter what happens. Make the best of the extra energy that you feel. You can use it for a sharper focus and to give a more energized rendition of your music. Let the sparks fly; enjoy the ride while it lasts. Within a short a time, you will notice that your Activation drops, possibly even below your Optimal range. Once that happens, you can stop.

When you're done, take a few moments to assimilate your experience. Then complete the evaluation in the box below. Be kind in your assessment; the first time most performers attempt this drill, they experience serious deterioration in their performance skills. It's similar to what happens in other stressful circumstances. I can assure you that things will get better as you get more accustomed to the process.

You can learn to perform your best because of that energy, not in spite of it. You'll be able to ride that wave as you allow the energy to work for you. Then it really gets to be fun and exciting. Once you embrace higher Activation levels in safe environments, you'll look for more and more challenging performance circumstances. That's a good sign that you're ready to move on.

		SIMULATION TRAINING			
		ACTIVATION LEVEL	ACTIVATION LEVEL	RATING	
DATE	TIME	BEFORE	START	(1–100)	COMMENTS

LEARN TO CENTER UP

Even for the most high-strung performers, there are times when the energy is just too low. Maybe you have a young child at home and arrive at concerts exhausted. Maybe you're on the last leg of a world tour or just feeling *down*. Every performer can find a use at some time for the *Centering Up* technique.

Centering Up will help you to quickly raise your energy, switch from left to right brain, and direct your increased energy from your Center to your focus point. It will give you the ability to raise your Activation within a few seconds, without running up and down stairs or even leaving the room.

Centering Up will take far less time to complete than Centering Down. If you are already proficient in Centering Down, you should be able to Center Up in fewer than twenty seconds.

Centering Up has the same basic starting position as Centering Down. Stand with your feet shoulder-width apart, with your arms hanging at your sides and your head up. Find a comfortable yet balanced position, with a slight bend in your knees. You want to feel grounded. Let's go over the process.

FORM YOUR CLEAR INTENTION You start the process by forming a clear idea of what you intend to do after you are Centered and Activated. Consciously choose what you will accomplish with the increased energy that you will channel. Your Clear Intention may be: "I am going to get up and play well at this rehearsal," or "Tonight I will be energized and give an exciting and inspiring performance."

PICK YOUR FOCUS POINT Choose a place where you will direct your high energy when you complete the Centering Up. Select a precise location at some distance away from you that is lower than eye level. You will keep your eyes open with a "hard focus" on that point for the remaining steps.

START RAPID BREATHING WHILE PUMPING HANDS After fixing your focus, begin breathing in and out through your mouth, rapidly and fully into your torso. As you do so, quickly pump your hands by opening and closing your fists. Your shoulders may rise and fall in the process; that's okay. Take three or more breaths, but stop the deep, rapid breathing before you get dizzy or hyperventilate. Go back to more regular breathing, but continue to breathe in and out through your mouth.

RELEASE UPPER-BODY TENSION The rapid breathing and pumping of your hands will tend to induce tension in your shoulders, arms, and hands. With this fourth step, simply release the tightness you may feel there, as well as in any other key muscles. Do this in one to three breaths.

BE AT YOUR CENTER Focus on your Center, two inches below your navel and two inches into your body. Get in touch with that place; direct your energy out of your left brain, down, and toward that more solid and grounded place.

REPEAT YOUR PROCESS CUE Use a cue that will excite you. Say it until you are feeling energized.

DIRECT YOUR ENERGY TO YOUR POINT From your center, summon the energy up through your body and out to your focus point. After you sense the connection and flow of energy from your Center to your focus point, Go For It!

When you start to practice Centering Up, it should take you between fifteen and thirty seconds. Use the log on the following page to keep track of your progress. The Process Goal is to be able to Center Up—to set up Optimal Performance—in less than ten seconds. Then you can use it instead of jumping rope or running the stairs.

CENTERING UP LOG

DATE	CLEAR INTENTION	KEY MUSCLES	PROCESS CUE	AT CENTER	NUMBER OF BREATHS	COMMENTS

DEVELOPING EASE

Ease under Pressure is the final category to address in your Advanced Training. Do you tend to try too hard and force things to happen under pressure? Or have you already learned the valuable skill of allowing things to just happen? Check your score from your Artist's Performance Survey and circle it below.

	LOW						MID-RANGE								HIGH	
Ease under	20	25	30	35	40	45	50	55	60	65	70	75	80	85	90	95	100
Pressure	Try Too Hard														Let It Go	

If you have a high score, make sure you take full advantage of your ability to Let It Go under pressure. If you have a low score, put away the hammer. You need to learn about the relationship between ease and your Activation.

If you've completed the Simulation Training drills, you know how to perform well with high positive energy. Now you will notice how increased Activation can result in greater ease: the higher your energy, the less effort you need. Once you experience that, you can Let It Go even more. Then it really takes off. That is the last piece of the puzzle. Hooray!

> *Less effort creates more results.*
> —ROBERT ANTHONY

Here is the training drill for the next few days. I strongly recommend that you do this one in private until you get the hang of it. The first few times are usually not pretty. This drill is not about accuracy; it is about ease and effortless power.

Choose a piece of music that is high-energy but relatively easy for you to perform. Put it on the music stand. If you need to tune, warm up, or practice the piece, please do so.

> *"All that you have learned hitherto,"* said the Master one day when he found nothing more to object to in my relaxed manner of drawing the bow, *"was only a preparation for loosing the shot."*
> —EUGEN HERRIGEL

Commit ahead of time that you are really going to Go For It.

Then leave the room and get your Activation far above your Optimal range. Pause to Center in less than five breaths. Allow the extra energy you feel to flow freely up and out from your Center to your focus point. Once you sense the connection, trust that you can ride that energy and let it power your performance. Get ready to Go For It and then Let It Go. See what happens.

> *The way to develop self-confidence is to do the thing you fear and get a record of successful experiences behind you.*
>
> —WILLIAM JENNINGS BRYAN

Your Activation will tend to come down within a minute or so. If you did not Let It Go, or it did not "take off" with power and ease, just give it another shot later in the day or tomorrow. When you're ready, set up the drill again. It usually happens after three or four attempts.

After each one, make some comments and observations in your log, including whether you were able to Go For It and Let It Go. When it does take off for you, just put a check and move on. Way to go! Pretty neat, huh?

EASE UNDER PRESSURE DRILLS

SELECTION OF MUSIC FOR DRILL: _____

	#1	#2	#3	#4	#5	#6	#7
ACTIVATION LEVEL	___	___	___	___	___	___	___
EFFORTLESS POWER	___	___	___	___	___	___	___
GO FOR IT?	___	___	___	___	___	___	___
LET IT GO?	___	___	___	___	___	___	___
TAKE OFF?	___	___	___	___	___	___	___
COMMENTS/OBSERVATIONS:	_____						

Building Courage

Great performers have guts. They love to take risks and hang it out on the edge. This is a strength you can develop. Here's how it works.

Think of ten events from the past when you were courageous—times when you took brave steps rather than following the path of fear. Reflect on your whole life, not just your work as a performer. Get in touch with those memories, how you handled the fear, and how your courageous choices were rewarded. Enter your events in the journal below.

COURAGE JOURNAL

OCCASION	THE FEAR I FACED	MY COURAGEOUS ACTION	RESULT
1. Senior Recital	Letting loved ones down	Letting positive feelings energize me	Great recital
2. Philly Orch.	My teacher was there	I went for it anyway	It was awesome!

COURAGE JOURNAL

OCCASION	THE FEAR I FACED	MY COURAGEOUS ACTION	RESULT
1. _____			
2. _____			
3. _____			
4. _____			
5. _____			
6. _____			
7. _____			
8. _____			
9. _____			
10. _____			

Now that you've recalled past courageous acts, I'd like you to look for opportunities each day to exercise your courage. Courage is like a muscle; you build it by using it. The log is a means of keeping track of your progress and successes.

Whenever you overcome fear and make the choice to do something courageous, enter it in your Courage Log, along with the result of that action. The log will be like bank book for a savings account. Each entry is a deposit. You are going to keep a record of each of your courageous steps as deposits into your account, keeping track of your investments and accumulating assets. Each act builds your account; it's a cumulative thing. It's not necessary or recommended that you do any incredibly heroic feats, like running into burning buildings to save people. You don't want to scare yourself to death. Start with small steps.

You could perform in front of friends, then colleagues, then teachers. On your own, you could perform challenging works that may have intimidated you in the past. Or you could just Go For It in certain difficult parts of a piece. The steps need not be restricted to performance situations, though. They may include the honest communication of your thoughts and feelings to friends or respected colleagues, or just calling a manager or conductor on the phone.

> *But screw up your courage to the sticking place and we'll not fail.*
> —WILLIAM SHAKESPEARE

After making twenty-one new entries in your Courage Log, give yourself a special gift, as a symbolic reminder of your total of thirty-one courageous acts. The reward is up to you, but it needs to be a tangible object, something that you can touch and see for a while (not food).

Decide ahead of time what your prize will be for taking the progressive steps required to receive it.

Congratulations. You've made it to the final stage of this book: the twenty-one-day Countdown. I wish you all the best. Have fun!

COURAGE JOURNAL
21 DAYS

EVENT/ SITUATION	FEAR	ACTION YOU TOOK	RESULT
1.			
2.			
3.			
4.			
5.			
6.			
7.			
8.			
9.			
10.			
11.			
12.			
13.			
14.			
15.			
16.			
17.			
18.			
19.			
20.			
21.			

6.

The Countdown
Get Ready for the Big Event

THE FOLLOWING COUNTDOWN is designed to work over a three-week period. As part of your training, you'll set up live performances at the end of each week, culminating with an important performance event. Ideally, you're flying to some big city for a major audition, competition or debut exactly three weeks from today. If there's nothing in your immediate calendar, set something up and make it as exciting as possible. Invite many people: friends, teachers, and colleagues. Sell tickets.

> *Easy is right.*
> *Begin right and you*
> *are easy. Continue easy*
> *and you are right.*
> *The right way to go easy*
> *is to forget the right way*
> *and forget that the*
> *going is easy.*
>
> —CHUANG-TZU

For each of the weeks, there's a prescribed agenda of activities to follow, including daily exercises and drills to complete and log entries to make. You'll need to devote at least 20–30 minutes a day to make the Countdown work well. If your schedule cannot accommodate this, you may want to wait until it can.

Although the Countdown is designed to begin with Day 21 as a Sunday, it can easily be adapted to other starting days. The calendar is on the following page. Take a look at it. You'll see that there's a full schedule of events for you over the next three weeks.

You will need to choose one special person—a friend, teacher, or mentor—to be your *sponsor* during the Countdown. This person should be, above all, supportive. He or she must also be available at three key points in the process (see schedule). Once you've found this person, refer him or her to the schedule and the sponsor's letter in the Appendix. Please don't read that page. It's for your sponsor, not you.

> *What you can do or dream you can do, begin it; boldness has genius, power and magic in it.*
> —JOHANN VON GOETHE

CALENDAR AND SCHEDULE OF EVENTS

Day 21. Check your schedule. Sign the contract.
Day 20. Start the Training Log. Perform run through.
Day 19. The Tapering process. Activation drill.
Day 18. Inventory your tools. Simulation drill.
Day 17. Refine your routine. Practice carbo-loading.
Day 16. The Attunement process. Take a field trip.
Day 15. First Mock Performance. You're on.*
Day 14. Rest and recovery. You're off.
Day 13. Reset goals. Set up Adversity Training.*
Day 12. Get ready. Your fight plan.
Day 11. What's your response?
Day 10. Win the fight. Your battle plan.
Day 9.   Correct interpretations. Your frustration.
Day 8.   Adverse Mock Performance. You're on.*
Day 7.   Rest and recovery. You're off.
Day 6.   Normal fears and doubts. Cue utilization.
Day 5.   Practice Optimal.
Day 4.   Shore up your courage.
Day 3.   Jettison nonessentials. Bide your time well.
Day 2.   Preserve your energy.
Day 1.   The Big Event.*

* Sponsor participation required

Are you ready? You can start as soon as you and your sponsor sign the contract. Once you begin on your journey, just keep going until you reach the end. You can count on achieving Optimal Performance in three weeks, if not sooner. Really. You know almost everything you need to perform your best; I'll tell you the rest on the way there. So, take a few Centering breaths, click your heels together three times, and smile. Here we go.

DAY 21: COMPLETE THE CONTRACT

CONTRACT

I, _____ , hereby agree that I will do
everything possible for the next 21 days to see how good I am.
I am ready to begin. It is up to me.
I also agree to enjoy the process as I observe myself getting better and
better.
I will further reward myself with _____ after
I have accomplished this goal.

_____   _____
(Date)   (Signed)

_____   _____
(Date)   (Sponsor*)

* Sponsor: see letter in Appendix

DAY 20: READY, SET, GO!

Again, the point of this Countdown is to get you ready for your Big Event, twenty days from now. With that in mind, there will be two *Mock Performances* during the Countdown, on Day 8 and Day 15. Start planning now what repertoire you'd like to use. For practicality's sake, it may be a good idea to keep it consistent through the course of the Mock Performances and the Big Event. It's your choice.

List these selections in your *Training Log* below. Include your goals for these pieces. Plan out your practice structure for performing them well at your first Mock Performance. As you go through the week, follow your practice plan, along with the recommended daily activities. You will want to keep track of your progress and insights in your daily Training Log.

Select the room or stage where you will be doing your first Mock Performance in six days. Make the necessary arrangement and make sure that your sponsor can be there. Have you thought about whom you're inviting to the Big Event? What about food and refreshments for your guests? It's all part of the Countdown.

Since the process is about harnessing and using energy effectively, you will want to start getting more sleep than usual. Drink at least four 8-ounce glasses of water every day. If you have an exercise regimen, please stay with it. If you're not currently on any fitness program, it would be a good idea to include a twenty-minute walk in your training structure.

> *Knowing is not enough,*
> *we must apply.*
> *Willing is not enough,*
> *we must do.*
> —JOHANN VON GOETHE

The training drill for today is to perform your repertoire and evaluate your technical and mental performance on a scale from 1 to 100, with 1 being horrible and 100 being outstanding. If there is anything you are not pleased with, revise your Goals and practice structure. If you can, go to bed early. Every day won't be this easy.

TRAINING LOG
DAY 20

Date: _____ Day of the Week: _____

Location of First Mock Performance: _____

Time: _____ Sponsor Contacted and Available? _____

Repertoire: 1 _____

2 _____ 3 _____

Evaluation: 1 _____

2 _____ 3 _____

Performance Goals

1 _____

2 _____

3 _____

Practice Structure

1 _____

2 _____

3 _____

Comments/Insights

_____

_____

_____

_____

_____

DAY 19: WE'RE NOT IN KANSAS ANYMORE

Have you made the necessary arrangements for your first Mock Performance in four days? Have you invited some guests? Will they help to raise your energy beyond your Optimal Activation range? I hope so.

As the day draws closer, it's time to prepare to use your energy to perform better and better through a process known as *Tapering*. It will get you physically and mentally ready to perform your best with high positive energy. It's a strategy used by Olympic athletes to Peak their energies at the right time. It involves backing off a high training plateau a week or two before competition, so they can begin the games with a massed amount of good energy to use.

> *The process of sleep . . . provides tremendous power. It restores, rejuvenates and energizes the body and brain.*
>
> —JAMES MAAS

The Tapering process requires that you begin by getting extra rest. Start entering the amount of sleep you are getting (including naps) in your daily Training Log. Proper rest is more important to your performance than you may think. It is critical.

This week, get eight or more hours of sleep a night. Next week you will need to get nine or more, and in your last week you will actually go for ten hours of combined sleep and naps each day. These recommendations are based on *Power Sleep,* by James Maas, Ph.D. Too many of us are working off a continual debt of too little sleep. If you do not wake up naturally in the morning, or if you need a cup of coffee to get going, maybe you are not getting enough sleep. If you feel drowsy in the afternoon, you might not be getting sufficient rest.

You need sleep for two reasons: to rest your body, and to allow for *REM (rapid eye movement) sleep,* in which you dream. You absolutely must get plenty of dream-rich REM sleep on a regular basis. If you were prevented from dreaming for a week or so, you would go nuts. At first, you might only experience difficulty paying attention or concentrating, but after a few days, you would start acting somewhat strangely. A few more days of this cruel experiment, and you would begin to exhibit an effect known to mental health professionals as *the Look.* In this state, your symptoms would range from confusion to paranoia and hypervigilance.

The point is that if you would like to have your full mental faculties available, you need to be working from good REM sleep. And get this: researchers have discovered that our best REM sleep comes between the seventh and eighth hour of continuous sleep.

I tested this for about a month. Instead of watching television until midnight and sleeping till the alarm went off at 7:00, I started going to bed at 10:00 and sleeping until 7:00. This was not a hard habit to establish. In a few days, I started waking up a bit ahead of the alarm. I noticed that my focus seemed sharper in the morning. Throughout the day, I was in a much better mood than the week before.

> *The Golden Rules of Sleep:*
> 1) *Get an adequate amount of sleep every night.*
> 2) *Establish a regular sleep schedule.*
> 3) *Get continuous sleep.*
> 4) *Make up for lost sleep.*

A month later, I gave two presentations at a college musical conference. I began each session by noting that my energy was usually up, but now it was even higher. More importantly, the quality of my energy was superior. Rather than that nasty edge of high anxiety, it was a solid and powerful. I felt that I was really on. These were two of the best presentations of my life.

Try it out for yourself. Get a couple extra hours of sleep in the next few days and you will see. Go to bed early, sleep in, or take a nap—without guilt.

Tonight, put your instrument somewhere near your bed (pianist and vocalists excepted). Put your music close by as well. Within a few seconds after you wake up tomorrow morning, get out of bed, quickly get your Activation up and into your Optimal range, and perform one of your pieces.

When you're done with the entire piece, and after you've really woken up, jot some notes in your log about the experience and how you can do it better next time.

TRAINING LOG
DAY 19

Date: _____ Day of the Week: _____

Amount of Sleep Last Night: _____

Length of Nap(s) Yesterday: _____

Glasses of Water Yesterday: _____

Length of Exercise/Walk: _____

Simulation Training Drills:

Selection of Music for Drill: _____

Time of Drill: _____

Activation Level before Activating: _____

After Activating: _____

Technique/Method for Activating: _____

Evaluation of Performance: _____

Comments: _____

_____

DAY 18: FOLLOW THE YELLOW BRICK ROAD

As you prepare for your first Mock Performance (in three days), it may be helpful to check your tools and see if they can be of assistance. Let's see, by now, you should have clearly envisioned Goals, be able to Center Up or Down in fewer than seven seconds, and be used to performing in your Optimal Activation range, focused within your boundary. And you should be doing so with ease.

Your outlook will take on extra significance in the next few days. What you think will be what you get. This is a good time for you to consider using *Affirmations*. These can be very helpful, especially when they are structured correctly. Rather than ultimatums, such as, "No one can play this better than me," or "I am the best in the world," you could say: "I am performing this piece better and better," or "My skills are getting stronger and stronger." Affirmations work best when they are true now and in the immediate future—so that you can say them with full conviction.

> *The thing always happens that you really believe in; and the belief in a thing makes it happen.*
>
> —FRANK LLOYD WRIGHT

If you found Mental Rehearsal to be helpful, I would encourage you to do a session today before you do the upcoming Simulation drill. Imagine all the important events before and during your performance. Start with your warming up, and then imagine yourself standing outside the door getting ready to go in.

If you experience any of the extra energy that you may feel during a real performance, that's great! It indicates that you are really into it. Simply do mentally what you would do in reality, namely Center. Actually go through the Centering process within your Mental Rehearsal session.

Once Centered, imagine yourself going in and performing just the way you would like. Envision it clearly, feel it fully, and hear the sound you would like to create. Make some notes in today's log about your Mental Rehearsal session and the degree to which it affects your performance in today's drill. Here it is.

Choose at least three of your repertoire pieces. Put them face down and shuffle them. The idea is to surprise yourself with an unknown. Get the rest of your performance room ready, but this time, turn your recorder on before you leave the room. Commit to Going For It when you come back in.

Get your Activation way above your Optimal range, then go back in and pick one of the pieces. Put it on the stand. Pause briefly to Center and then allow the energy to flow.

Trust it and Let It Go. Perform the entire piece. When you are done, make some comments on the tape before you turn it off and enter your insights in your log. If you are not pleased with the results, feel free to take another shot at it later in the day.

Make notes in your log about your Concentration before and during the drill. Mention what distracted you or prevented you from being mentally quiet and fully absorbed in the here and now. Rate your presence and intensity of focus, 1 being totally distracted and 100 being one-pointed concentration.

You will have numerous opportunities over the next few days to refine your Recovery Strategy and get even better at moving past mistakes. Rate yourself on your recovery time during the drill, with 1 being much too long and 100 being instantaneously. Consider what may still keep you from getting back on track fast. Keep notes on your progress.

TRAINING LOG
DAY 18

Date: _____ Day of the Week: _____

Amount of Sleep Last Night: _____

Length of Nap(s) Yesterday: _____

Glasses of Water Yesterday: _____

Length of Exercise/Walk: _____

Affirmations: _____

_____

_____

Mental Rehearsal Sessions: _____

_____

_____

Simulation Training Drills

Mental Quiet   _____ _____ _____

Here and Now   _____ _____ _____

Intensity of Focus   _____ _____ _____

Recovery   _____ _____ _____

Comments/Insights: _____

_____

DAY 17: MAKE YOUR ROUTINE A ROUTINE

It's time now to focus on refining your pre-event routine, the physical and mental things you do fifteen to thirty minutes before you go on. In the following log, please write out the routine that sets you up to perform well. See the Attentional Plan on page 79 for a refresher. Commit to sticking with this sequence today, tomorrow and for your first Mock Performance in two days.

As you get closer to that performance, consider what you are eating. This will provide energy that you will be using to perform. Two days before an event, it is very important that you *carbo-load*. In other words, eat a simple pasta meal, but without a lot of sausage or spice. You will be working from that energy base in two days.

Tonight's sleep is important. The sleep you get tonight will have more of an impact on your performance than the sleep you get tomorrow night. That is why you need to prepare for a good night's rest tonight.

After your pasta meal, try to restrict the amount of sugar you take in, and try not to drink anything but water. I recommend that you even stop drinking water two or three hours before you go to bed. Start preparing for a good night's rest about an hour before you would like to fall asleep.

> *Repetition of the right physical, mental and emotional habits eventually brings them under automatic control. Conscious awareness and targeted energy expenditure will gradually give way to automatic rituals . . . that keep you in balance.*
>
> —JAMES LOEHR

Keep your activities low-key. Get into bed and watch a boring television show or, better yet, read something that will make you sleepy. Then turn off the lights and allow yourself several minutes to drift off. If you are still awake after fifteen or twenty minutes, slowly go through your entire body and make sure that you are very relaxed and comfortable.

This is not the time to do any Mental Rehearsal of your performance. Just lay there and be as mellow as possible. Try to not get up or turn on the lights or the TV. You will still get vital rest, even if you do not fall asleep as soon as you would like. Pleasant dreams.

TRAINING LOG
DAY 17

Date: _____ Day of the Week: _____

Amount of Sleep Last Night: _____

Length of Nap(s) Yesterday: _____

Glasses of Water Yesterday: _____

Length of Exercise/Walk: _____

Routine:_____

_____

_____

_____

Affirmations:_____

_____

_____

Pasta Meal: _____

Comments/Insights: _____

Go to Bed Early. Pleasant dreams.

DAY 16: GET ATTUNED

If at all possible, take the following field trip today. Go to the room, stage, or hall where you will be doing your first Mock Performance. This critical site visit should enable you to get a sense of ownership and control over the physical surroundings where you will create an Optimal Performance. Check out the locations where you will be warming up, waiting, and Centering before you go in. This is called the *Attunement process.*

As you walk in revise your *Attentional Plan.* As you go from the door into your performance space, decide where you will put your Attention. As you get to your starting place, look all around and then pick out your focus point. It remains advisable that these be lower than eye level. Now Center and imagine yourself performing just the way you would like it to go. Take your time.

When you are pleased with what you see, hear, and feel, take a walk around the room. If you can, walk around its entire perimeter. Pause at different spots, look back to where you will be performing, and imagine yourself up there, doing great and enjoying the process. Then get to a spot as far away as possible from your starting place but where you are still able to see it. A seat in the back row would be ideal.

Once you are there, Center again, then look around and take it all in. Get a sense of control over everything you see. Then focus on where you will be standing or sitting for your perform-ance. Imagine yourself there in the spotlight. See yourself starting out well. Hear your beautiful sound going out into the space. Notice how good you

> *The moment of enlightenment is when a person's dreams of success become images of probabilities.*
>
> —VIC BRADEN

feel in this space. Embrace it so you can make it work for you and your upcoming performance. Then write about Attunement and your latest insights in your log.

Contact your sponsor today to confirm that he or she will be there for tomorrow's performance. Are you ready? The answer is: Yes.

TRAINING LOG
DAY 17

Date: _____ Day of the Week: _____

Amount of Sleep Last Night: _____

Length of Nap(s) Yesterday: _____

Glasses of Water Yesterday: _____

Length of Exercise/Walk: _____

Attunement Process: _____

_____

_____

Insights: _____

_____

_____

Go to Bed Early. Pleasant dreams.

DAY 15: TODAY'S THE DAY

Welcome to the day of your first Mock Performance. For breakfast, stick to what you have been eating for the past few mornings. This is not your cue to go out for pancakes, bacon, sausage, hash browns, a Western omelette, and a pot of coffee. It's a good time to eat something fairly simple—just cereal or just fruits. I suggest fruit, especially bananas, and keep on hydrating with water.

If your performance is in the morning, make sure that you do not eat too much just before you go in. It may take away your energy. If you feel as though you're going to be over-activated and have too much nervous energy, you may want to have something in your stomach that will absorb the extra energy. Since gastric acid will probably be released in your stomach under the pressure, it may be helpful to take something with you, like another banana, a bran muffin, or a plain bagel. Any of those will absorb the acid.

> *On the day
> I'm performing,
> I don't hear
> anything anyone
> says to me.*
> —LUCIANO PAVAROTTI

If your performance is later in the day or evening, try to stay with your usual eating routines, erring on the side of less rather than more. Keep hydrating and remember that you will be working mostly off the good energy from your carbo-loading two nights ago.

It's normal to experience dramatic drops in energy before performances. There is no reason to freak out about it or eat six candy bars. Know that your energy will come back up again before you go on. By then, you'll probably also experience a surge of adrenaline. Just continue to bide your time well.

If you are performing in the afternoon, I would encourage you not to take a nap. Be careful about putting your body into a sleep pattern that will dramatically drop your Activation. If you absolutely need to nap, please keep it less than thirty minutes, and not within an hour or two of your performance. When you do wake up, make sure that after you get up, you take a brisk walk, preferably in the fresh air.

TRAINING LOG
DAY 15

Date: _____ Day of the Week: _____
Amount of Sleep Last Night: _____
Length of Nap(s) Yesterday: _____
Glasses of Water Yesterday: _____
Length of Exercise/Walk: _____

Here's the drill. Make sure that your sponsor is in a comfortable place to observe your every movement and clearly hear your sound. Hit the "record" button on your tape recorder before you leave the room. Get your Activation above your Optimal Activation range and pause briefly outside the room to Center. Then enter the room and perform the first part of the first piece. Then Center again and perform the first part of the second piece. After a brief pause to Center again, play the entire third piece.

When you've finished, make some comments on tape. Mention what you did well and what you need to improve next time. Complete the evaluation and write out your insights. Have your sponsor complete an evaluation as well. Express your gratitude to your sponsor in a meaningful way.

> *Why not go out on a limb? Isn't that where the fruit is?*
>
> —FRANK SCULLY

FIRST MOCK PERFORMANCE

Date: _____ Time: _____ Location: _____

Part/Piece/ Excerpt	Rating	Strengths	Areas to Improve
_____	_____	_____	_____
_____	_____	_____	_____
_____	_____	_____	_____

Comments/Insights: _____
_____
_____
_____

Sponsor: _____

Part/Piece/ Excerpt	Rating	Observations
_____	_____	_____
_____	_____	_____
_____	_____	_____

Comments: _____

_____

DAY 14: REST AND RECOVERY

Take a break. If possible, take the entire day off. You deserve it. If you'd like to do anything, go out and treat yourself to a reward that will remind you of what you have accomplished thus far. Make sure you get some extra rest. Take a nap without guilt. If you're going to do something, let it be an activity that you truly enjoy, but something that does not require a lot of energy. Learn to rest, recover, and nurture yourself as you prepare for the next battle.

DAY 13: ONCE MORE UNTO THE BREACH DEAR FRIENDS

Welcome back. I hope that you're rested and refreshed. Before we move forward, take a brief look back on last week's accomplishments and especially your first Mock Performance. Consider what you did well and what can you do better. Outline your goals for this weekend's performance in your Training Log.

> *You may have to fight a battle more than once to win it.*
>
> —MARGARET THATCHER

This week, drink six glasses of water each day and try to eat as healthy a diet as possible. If possible, get at least eight or nine hours of sleep. You'll be going through Adversity Training at the end of this week. It's not going to be easy. Make sure that your sponsor has read the letter and is available to set up for your Adverse Mock Performance.

One summer I attended an international music competition at the Eastman School in Rochester. During the semifinal round, one of the players was in the middle of a final diminuendo; she was playing really softly. Not far from the stage, there was evidently a practice room where a trumpet player started to warm up. Everyone in the concert hall heard it immediately; it was *loud*. Fortunately, the musician kept her focus and went right on playing. She finished the piece as if nothing had happened. The audience and judges let her know they were impressed.

With the assistance of your sponsor, we will conspire, via the sponsor's letter in the Appendix, to set up a series of interesting challenges for you to overcome. If you can take it seriously enough, you can learn a great deal about yourself from this experience. To paraphrase the saying, "Circumstances reveal the man or woman." The goal of the Adversity drill is for you to be able to perform well, *no matter what*.

You have little or no control over some of the unfortunate things that may happen in live performance situations. Does your performance take a hit under adverse circumstances? Do you respond as a helpless victim and feel sorry for yourself? Do you look to blame someone else for the injustice? Or do you focus on what you need to do, *no matter what*?

No matter what the circumstances are, *no matter what* anybody does. Do you stay focused on your process and

> *Challenges make you discover things about yourself that you never really knew. That's what makes the instrument stretch, what makes you go beyond the norm.*
>
> —CICELY TYSON

do well, *no matter what*? Within the Adversity experience, you'll discover your own best responses to potentially distracting or disturbing events. Once you have that, you'll be prepared for anything. Are you ready?

TRAINING LOG
DAY 13

Date: _____ Day of the Week: _____
Amount of Sleep Last Night: _____
Length of Nap(s) Yesterday: _____

Glasses of Water Yesterday: _____

Length of Exercise/Walk: _____·_____

Location of Adverse Mock Performance: _____

Time: _____ Sponsor/Replacement: _____

Performance Goals:_____

_____

Practice Structure:_____

_____

Insights:_____

_____

_____

DAY 12: GET READY TO FIGHT

I once worked with a mezzo-soprano from Philadelphia. Let's call her Stephanie. She had recently failed a regional competition, and complained that she usually felt like an underdog when she came to New York to audition. Stephanie was not doing very well. I suggested that she think about fighting. She did not like the idea.

The concept of fighting didn't feel good to her. It was "coming from too far out in left field." She did not want to watch any *Rocky* movies. As the next Metropolitan Opera competition approached and Stephanie's fears and doubts surfaced, she came to understand that the real fight was on the inside. Three days before the competition, she was barraged by a chorus of negative voices warning of potential doom and disaster.

It would require a constant struggle to stay on top of her negative voices, or they would "pop in," take control, and wear her down. She had to monitor her own thoughts, ever-vigilant in the final days leading up to the bigger contest. The closer the event, the more Stephanie would need to fight to stay on top of her fears and doubts and negative voices.

I told her to imagine that she was offstage putting boxing gloves on, getting geared up and ready for her fight. The bell was about to ring. Ding! Round One. She put her guard up and used her energy to fight. She won the district competition, then the state, then the regional competition. She battled her way through the worst enemies—inside—and emerged victorious.

Stephanie maintains that she does not like to fight. We both recognize that it's hard for most performers to embrace the concept. But you can develop your toughness by constantly looking for challenges, hoping that circumstances will bring pressure to bear on you. And when they do, don't say: "Oh, this is terrible." Say: "Come on, bring it on!"

In today's log, please write out some thoughts on your fight plan for your upcoming battles. The idea is to have your guard up before you get into hostile territory, and keep it up until you're done. Remember Stephanie's experience. Protect yourself at all times; it is a fight. I did not design the system; I just know what works. Victims tend to lose. Fighters tend to win.

> *We shall go on to the end . . . we shall fight with growing confidence . . . we shall defend our island, whatever the cost shall be.*
>
> —SIR WINSTON CHURCHILL

For the next few days, practice your repertoire however you choose. My suggestion is to perform it in increasingly challenging circumstances. If you were in New York, I'd have you performing at least once on a subway platform. Challenge yourself.

TRAINING LOG
DAY 12

Date: _____ Day of the Week: _____

Amount of Sleep Last Night: _____

Length of Nap(s) Yesterday: _____

Glasses of Water Yesterday: _____

Length of Exercise/Walk: _____

Fight Plan: _____

_____

_____

Comments:_____

_____

Insights:_____

_____

DAY 11: WHAT'S YOUR RESPONSE?

In 1984 the U.S. Volleyball Team was preparing for the Olympics. There were several individual "stars" and certain cliques within the team. Some of the players would not set other players up for spikes. They passed the ball off to their friends instead. They did not play like a team. There was a lot of dissension, blaming, and whining by the players. The coaches decided to take them on the Outward Bound program.

> *A problem is a chance for you to do your best.*
> —DUKE ELLINGTON

Outward Bound is a two-week wilderness experience that helps people build confidence in themselves and others. The program teaches survival skills and self-reliance, and presents tough situations that can only be solved through teamwork. For the U.S. Volleyball Team, it must have been effective: the team won the gold.

I recommend Outward Bound or any similar course to you. I went through the army's Ranger School, which was two months long and very challenging. In fact, it was a nasty ordeal from beginning to end. But it did engender in me a determination to accomplish my "mission" under extreme circumstances. Remember the expression: "What does not kill you makes you stronger."

> *If you want the rainbow, you gotta put up with the rain.*
> —DOLLY PARTON

I remember finishing and thinking that if I had to walk from Miami to Seattle, I could do it. I'd probably hate it, but I could do it. There was no doubt in my mind; it would just be a matter of time before I got to Seattle. Although I would never want to go through it again, Ranger School taught me several valuable lessons that I would like to share with you. You can receive the benefits without all the nonsense and unnecessary pain.

By now, your sponsor should have some interesting challenges ready to pose for you at this weekend's Adverse Mock Performance. Your job will be to make the best of it. Be prepared to perform all three repertoire selections. There may be sight-reading as well. The important thing is not whether you make mistakes or not. If your sponsor follows the instructions in my letter (in the Appendix) and sets it up right, you will make mistakes. That's not the point. The important thing is how you respond to the circumstances.

Here are some things you will want to keep in mind. By now, you should be able to Center in a few breaths. Whenever you have a few moments, Center, or at least pause to make sure that your key muscles are relaxed. Then bring your focus back on the process and your task at hand.

After the bell has rung and you're coming out of your corner, put your guard up and be ready for anything. The idea is to make the best of whatever circumstances present themselves. Hang in there; fight a good battle. Keep your guard up until you are safely back in your dressing room.

> *When written in Chinese, the word "crisis" is composed of two characters. One represents danger, and the other opportunity.*
>
> —JOHN F. KENNEDY

Then the question will be, how did you respond? Was it more like a helpless victim of the unfortunate situation, unable to get past the circumstances? If this resulted in a mistake, and you were unable to recover, did it set up a domino effect or a train wreck?

On the other hand, it you accepted the challenge as an opportunity to get tougher, you profited from the experience. You can then go into every subsequent performance in your career with the reasonable expectancy that you are going to do well, *no matter what.* Remember to bring all your other strengths and allies as well: your talent, your courage, your focus, your training and experience. It's up to you. Make it happen.

The drill for today is to consider your successful responses to adverse circumstances in your career. What are your best options when unexpected and unfortunate things happen? In your log, formulate your plan for responding Optimally during your Adverse Mock Performance. Then Mentally Rehearse various scenarios that challenge you. Make sure that you can imagine yourself responding well to all of them.

TRAINING LOG
DAY 11

Date: _____ Day of the Week: _____

Amount of Sleep Last Night: _____

Length of Nap(s) Yesterday: _____

Glasses of Water Yesterday: _____

Length of Exercise/Walk: _____

Previous Challenges: What You Did to Respond

_____

_____

_____

_____

Challenge: How You Could Respond

_____

_____

Mental Rehearsal Sessions: _____

_____

Comments/Insights:_____

_____

DAY 10: WIN THE FIGHT

Many of my ideas come from the army, where battle-tested formulas have proven effective in serious competition. The following military strategy is extremely effective and employs seven principles: *Objective, Mass, Economy of Resources, Security, Offensive, Momentum,* and *Unity.* These are the ways to win or prevail under Adversity. Whether you're in combat or performing a challenging repertoire under the worst possible conditions, these principles can help you. Study and understand them.

The Objective is your *Mission.* That is why Centering begins by forming a Clear Intention of what you are going to do. Always start with your Mission clearly in mind and create Process Cues that will help you accomplish that mission.

The principle of *Mass* means that you accumulate more than sufficient resources and energy before big events. This is why the Tapering process is so important to learn and practice.

Economy of Resources relates to your use of energy. Having accumulated as much energy as possible, you need to spend it wisely before and during your performance. If you anticipate the demands on your Concentration and plan out your Attentional expenditures, you will have sufficient energy to stay focused through the last note.

The principle of *Security* means that you put your guard up before you go into hostile surroundings and keep it up until you're done. If your boundary has been helpful, this is the time to use it. People may be taking shots at you; it's not likely to be a friendly environment. As they say in boxing, "Protect yourself at all times." No kidding.

Offensive means that you go on the attack. That is why you need to summon your courage and commit to Going For It *before* you get in the heat of battle. Whether it's warfare or a live broadcast of your exposed entrance, tentativeness does not work. You must Go For It.

The principle of *Momentum* says that if you stay with the process, the energy will pick up a speed of its own. Then it requires less effort and seems easier. If you are able to finally Let It

> *In war there is no second prize for the runner-up.*
>
> —GENERAL OMAR BRADLEY

Go at that point, your performance will truly take off. You can watch the sparks start to fly.

Unity is the singular focus required to do your best. If you are divided against yourself, you will lose—or at least shoot yourself in the foot. Focus on accomplishing your mission. Do not assist your opponent or fall victim to your hostile environment. Be your own best ally. Stay focused on completing your mission, *no matter what.*

Since you can count on potentially distracting and disturbing events happening during your Adverse Mock Performance in two days, you can make good use of these principles. In your log, write out your battle plan for accomplishing your Mission, *no matter what.*

TRAINING LOG
DAY 10

Date: _____ Day of the Week: _____

Amount of Sleep Last Night: _____

Length of Nap(s) Yesterday: _____

Glasses of Water Yesterday: _____

Length of Exercise/Walk: _____

Pasta Meal This Evening: _____

Plan for Adverse Mock Performance

Mission: _____

Mass: _____

_____

Economy of Resources: _____

_____

Security: _____

_____

Offensive: _____

_____

Momentum: _____

_____

Unity: _____

_____

DAY 9: GET INTO A GOOD HEAD

In the last day or two before big performances, artists are subject to a little-known phenomenon called the *Zeigarnik Effect*. It has to do with the frustration that you may feel in this sensitive time. As you get closer to achieving your goal, rather than decreasing, your frustration will probably increase.

> *Optimism and humor are the grease and glue of life. Without both of them, we would never have survived our captivity.*
>
> —FORMER POW
> PHILIP BUTLER

What this means is that you should be aware of your frustration levels as you near your performance. Also notice what you're doing with that energy. Frustration is not necessarily bad, but the tendency is to let the frustration get out of control or to direct it inappropriately. In fact, if you try, you can turn that frustration energy into even greater focus and determination to accomplish your Mission.

At this point it's also important that you reach the correct interpretation of external circumstances and internal perceptions. As your performance comes closer and the stress increases, you may become more aware of otherwise inconsequential events and sensations. Suddenly, things like how someone greets you or the way your instrument feels in the greenroom can take on extra significance and may be interpreted the wrong way.

> *There is nothing either good or bad but thinking makes it so*
> —SHAKESPEARE

Whatever the external circumstance or internal perception, you need to interpret it correctly. Let me help. Whatever it is, it means that you're going to perform well. Whether it is the way someone says hello to you on your way to the stage, or feeling something in your knee, it all means the same thing: it means that you are going to do well. Give this and your energy some thought today as you go about your daily activities, and write out your insights in your log.

Contact your sponsor to make sure that everything's set for the fun and games tomorrow.

TRAINING LOG
DAY 9

Date: _____ Day of the Week: _____

Amount of Sleep Last Night: _____

Length of Nap(s) Yesterday: _____

Glasses of Water Yesterday: _____

Length of Exercise/Walk: _____

Your Frustration Levels: _____

_____

Events and Interpretations: _____

_____

Comments/Insights: _____

_____

Contact Your Sponsor: _____

DAY 8: ADVERSITY SIMULATION

The drill is simple. Turn on your recording device. Then follow your sponsor's directions and make the best of it. When you've finished, make some comments on tape. In your log, mention what you did well and what you need to improve. Complete the evaluation and also ask your sponsor to complete one. Afterwards, please convey your gratitude to your sponsor.

ADVERSE MOCK PERFORMANCE

Date: _____ Time: _____ Location: _____

Part/Piece/Excerpt	Rating	Strengths	Areas to Improve
_____	_____	_____	_____
_____	_____	_____	_____
_____	_____	_____	_____
_____	_____	_____	_____

Comments/Insights: _____

_____

_____

Sponsor: _____

Part/Piece/Excerpt	Rating	Comments
_____	_____	_____
_____	_____	_____
_____	_____	_____
_____	_____	_____ _____

TRAINING LOG
DAY 8

Date: _____ Day of the Week: _____

Amount of Sleep Last Night: _____

Length of Nap(s) Yesterday: _____

Glasses of Water Yesterday: _____

Length of Exercise/Walk: _____

DAY 7: REST AND RECOVERY

Take a break. If possible, take the entire day off. You deserve it. If you'd like to do anything special today, please do. If you haven't done it already, get a nice present for your sponsor. Treat yourself as well to a reward that will remind you of what you've accomplished so far. Otherwise, rest and nurture yourself to prepare for your next battle.

DAY 6: ONCE MORE WITH FEELING

At this point, it is important that we raise the bar again. Have you set up your final Mock Performance for the end of the week? Have you invited several friends, colleagues, and possibly your teacher to the Big Event? If the thought of that causes you worry or concern in any way, there's a name for the phenomenon and a strategy to make use of it.

The phenomenon is called *normal fears and doubts*. If your performance in five days' time in front of your select others is important to you, it's very normal to have fears and doubts. There are never any guarantees with live performances, and since the technical skills are not necessarily easy to do even under relaxed circumstances, it's normal to experience fears and doubts; it's just not helpful.

You're walking down the street or riding in your car before an important performance and you get hit with a "zinger." All of a sudden, you think: "What if I screw up in front of my teacher?" or "What if I forget one of the parts?" or "I hope I don't miss the high note!" These zingers zap performers out of the blue. Normal fears and doubts tend to increase as you get closer to your target dates.

> *Experience is not what happens to you; it is what you do with what happens to you.*
> —ALDOUS HUXLEY

You're on your way to a rehearsal and you think: "I hope I don't mess up on that hard part." Then you think: "If I do that again, they're going to think that I can't do it." That may soon lead to: "If that happens, it will make it even harder for me to do in the first performance. Then they will think that I can't. . . . " The progression occurs very quickly. If you allow it to continue, it will snowball in the wrong direction. It may be normal, but it does not serve you in any way.

When you get zapped by a zinger, you can either allow the progression to quickly take you to imagining the worst, or you can start making more positive use of the zingers. The strategy for handling the fears and doubts is known as *Cue Utilization*. It starts with the zinger or cue and ends up with you being in a much better place.

> *It's normal to experience fears and doubts, it's just not helpful.*

The process begins when you label the zinger as normal fear and doubt. Just say to yourself: "Ah, normal fear and doubt." As you label it, you distance yourself from it. Then you can deal with it more objectively rather than getting caught up in the middle of your snowballing fears and doubts. The process of labeling the fears and doubts as normal and objectifying them will set you up to use the inevitable zingers as cues for producing more positive results.

Once you label the zinger as normal fear and doubt, you have three main options. If you're concerned about a certain part in the music and experience a zinger, think about what you need to do to perform that part well. Say that as a Process Cue to yourself and imagine performing it just the way you would like it to go.

> *Go back to your Highlight Films of times when you nailed it.*

If you get a visual zinger, in which you see yourself making a mistake, go back in your mind to images of some of your best performances of that part. We will call them your Highlight Films.

Rather than picturing things that could go wrong, go back to times when you nailed it. Remember what it looked like, how you felt, and what it sounded like. Immerse yourself in a right-brain experience. Hang out there for a few seconds or longer.

Then recall another occasion when you performed it well. Again, immerse yourself in a sensory experience: look around the stage or room, feel how you felt, and hear the sound you produced. Remember how good you were. Then move to another Highlight Film.

After that, go back to what you had been doing about a minute ago, before you got zapped.

If the zinger brings up circumstances for which you have no Highlight Films, then keep in mind that they are merely hypothetical constructs. They do not exist in reality, they're simply normal fears and doubts of what could go wrong. Consider what you've worried about in the past. The likely fact is that the vast majority, if not all of them, never happened. You need to see that normal fears and doubts are irrational. They will not exist in reality unless you make them happen.

That's Cue Utilization. You will be afforded many opportunities to practice this strategy and you will get better at turning zingers into positive results. Please keep track of your progress in your Training Log.

TRAINING LOG
DAY 6

Date: _____ Day of the Week: _____

Amount of Sleep Last Night: _____

Length of Nap(s) Yesterday: _____

Glasses of Water Yesterday: _____

Length of Exercise/Walk: _____

What Did You Get for Your Sponsor? _____

_____

What Was Your Reward for Last Week's Efforts? _____

_____

Cue Utilization

Normal Fear and Doubt (Zinger)   Strategy Used

_____   _____

_____   _____

_____   _____

_____   _____

Comments/Insights: _____

_____

_____

_____

DAY 5: ALMOST THERE

In my experience of working with Juilliard students and Fellows at the New World Symphony, I found that many of them were perfectionists. Their perfectionism had served a purpose at a certain point earlier in their learning and development, but more recently had undermined their ability to perform Optimally under pressure. Their expectancy of performing absolutely flawlessly under extreme stress prevented them from performing even close to their ability when they really needed to, as in juries and auditions.

Rather than expecting a perfect performance, a more functional Process Goal would be that of performing "pretty well." Once you are under pressure, you will appreciate a small cushion, from 3 to 7 percent off your absolute best: not perfect, not even 98 percent, but 93 percent or above. Not bad. Anything above that is icing on the cake.

> *The goal is to perform Optimally, not perfectly.*

You're in control of your activation and ease, self-talk, normal fears and doubts—everything from the skin in. Direct your singular focus to your process and the task at hand. You can control your energy, your thoughts and your expectations. It's important at this point that you rehearse what you are going to do in five days the way you expect to do it—Optimally but not perfectly.

Here's the situation. Assume that you're in the last round of dives in the springboard competition in the Olympics. Most of the divers know where they rank by checking their scores on the leader board. Let's assume that one of the finalists is about to do a front three-and-a-half somersault. For the last three months of practice, he did the dive three or four times a day, five days a week. If he was judged on those dives in practice, day in and day out, he would usually score around 8 or 9. Once in a while, he might even get a $9^1/2$, but that was rare.

As he is preparing to do the dive in the Olympics, he knows what scores he needs in order to win or at least get a medal. The question is, should he try to do the dive for eights or nines, or try to do it for tens?

If he tries to do it for tens, he will need to do it differently from how he is accustomed to doing it. He will have to jump a little higher, spin a little faster, and come out a little sooner in order to line it up perfectly. Unfortunately, if he does jump higher, spin faster, and come out sooner, he will be in an unfamiliar place. That is not where he should be under extreme pressure. It will cause him to go past his rotation, and he'll wind up on his back. I've seen too many divers who went for tens in critical situations and ended up with threes. They had unwisely attempted something under extreme circumstances that they had not rehearsed.

The divers who drop from medal contention to finishing fifth or sixth are the ones who put themselves in unfamiliar places under pressure. Believe me, trying to do extra-specially well or perfectly under high stress will destroy your best efforts.

If a diver tries to do it for eight-and-a-halfs or nines, he will come off the board in a familiar position, kick out of the somersault at the usual place, and line up the entry just as he has done all those times in practice. If he's extra-clean on his entry and catches the water just right, the judges may give him a $9^1/2$, maybe even a 10.

That's what we're looking for when you're performing under stress. I'd rather have you do it pretty well under that pressure in a way that is familiar, the way you rehearsed it. This approach wins gold medals, auditions, and competitions of all kinds.

In your training drills today, practice performing the way you intend to at the Big Event. Go through your routine and rehearse everything you're going to do. Now's the time to try going for $9^1/2$'s and 10's.

TRAINING LOG
DAY 5

Date: _____ Day of the Week: _____

Amount of Sleep Last Night: _____

Length of Nap(s) Yesterday: _____

Glasses of Water Yesterday: _____

Length of Exercise/Walk: _____

Cue Utilization: _____

_____

Simulation Training Drills: _____

_____

Comments/Insights: _____

_____

_____

DAY 4: HANG IN THERE

Three days away from your Big Event, it's important to continue the Tapering process and plan on getting more rest. This is the time to do more Mental Rehearsals and short training drills, and less physical and technical practice. This is when you cut back even more; you need to preserve your chops and your good energy for the right time.

You need as much of that energy as you can accumulate and bring with you into your performance. Then you will be able to perform with effortless power. You need to guard your time more closely in these final days of the Countdown process. If you can suspend nonessential projects and put off unnecessary meetings until after your upcoming performance, it would be helpful.

> *Hold the sound or image in your mind of performing just the way you would like to.*

You have a fight coming up in a few days. You want to be prepared to go in and give it your best shot. Are you ready? If you are not sure, there are a few things you might consider doing today or tomorrow. One is to watch a *Rocky* or *Rambo* movie and relate it to your upcoming battle. If these turn you off, you could rent any video or listen to any music that really inspires you.

You'll need to shore up your courage. If you've started a Courage Log, this would be a good time to review your entries. During the next few days, you will need to use your courage to commit to Go For It.

Clearly envision what you intend to do during your upcoming performance. Remember, in the days right before important events, normal fears and doubts tend to increase and multiply. One of the best things you can do, in addition to Cue Utilization, is to hold the sound or image in your mind of performing just the way you would like.

Develop the mental discipline over the next few days to keep only positive thoughts in your mind. Keep focused on performing Optimally. Reinforce that with affirmations and positive imagery. You need to convince yourself that you are going to perform the way you intend to. This needs to become clearer as the final day approaches. It will become increasingly important that you are convinced that you are going to perform well.

Become vigilant in these next days about the contents of your mind. It's crucial that you remain focused on your process and what you need to do. Allow only positive feelings, words, images, and sounds in your mind. Hold on to those as much as you are able; they will serve you well when the time comes.

This will be your last simulation training drill before your live performance. Have you invited your friends and colleagues yet? How about your teacher? As you do the drill today, imagine them sitting in front of you. If that raises your Activation, great! Get as close as you can to the way you will probably feel in a few days as you walk into the room. You know what to do.

TRAINING LOG
DAY 4

Date: _____ Day of the Week: _____

Amount of Sleep Last Night: _____

Length of Nap(s) Yesterday: _____

Glasses of Water Yesterday: _____

Length of Exercise/Walk: _____

Non-Essential Projects/Events: _____

Simulation Training Drill: _____

Mental Rehearsals: _____

_____

Affirmations: _____

_____

Comments/Insights: _____

_____

DAY 3: WHOA

You now have two days until your performance. As you get nearer, continue to pay close attention to accumulating good energy by doing less and resting more. It's critical that you go into your performance fresh and ready to deal effectively with whatever may happen. You will not be doing any more simulation drills this week.

You've done the work, so now is the time to start enjoying the rewards of your labors. Two days before the college boards is not the time to take out the trigonometry books. At this point, wherever you are technically is the level you need to accept, so you can direct your attention to the more important matter: performing well with what you have. Put the études and technical books away, you need to go in there with as much good energy as possible.

> *Jettison activities that are not essential to your performing well.*

It's also a good idea from this point on to jettison activities that are not essential to your performing well. This would be anything or anyone that consumes your precious energy or time in the next two days.

That is not to say that you should spend your time practicing. One of the most challenging aspects of the last forty-eight hours is passing the time without expending a lot of energy. It's not always easy sitting on top of that much energy, even if it's good energy. Learning how to bide your time efficiently without burning off energy is an essential skill. So what do you do with the extra time you have carved out of your busy schedule?

Maybe there's a good book you've wanted to read lately. Are there any good movies you've been meaning to see? Now is the time. May I recommend a comedy? You need to keep your sense of humor and take it with you when you go in to perform in a couple days. Your performance is too important to take too seriously.

I would not recommend a visit to a museum. Being on your feet that much would take too much energy. I'd suggest a relatively short walk instead. One thing you can do today is put together your *Warm Fuzzy Bag*. Besides water and snacks, your Warm Fuzzy Bag should include anything that will help you pass the time, if you need to, before you perform. You might consider comfortable slippers, a magazine or novel, or even a stuffed animal. Whatever you'd like. Always be prepared for delays.

In the meantime, if you absolutely need to work on something in one of the pieces, just warm up and perform for short periods of time. I'd rather that you spend your limited practice time today doing your final Mental Rehearsals. One of those will preferably be at the same time of day as your performance. You will also want to go through all the important events leading up to your performance: such as warming up, your pre-event routine, and Centering. Imagine your performance from beginning to end just the way you would like it to look, feel, and sound. Then go out and have some pasta and go to bed early.

TRAINING LOG
DAY 3

Date: _____ Day of the Week: _____

Amount of Sleep Last Night: _____

Length of Nap(s) Yesterday: _____

Glasses of Water Yesterday: _____

Length of Exercise/Walk: _____

Time-Consuming Activities That Preserve Your Energy: _____

_____

Carbo-Loading Meal: _____

Mental Rehearsals: _____

_____

Contents of Warm Fuzzy Bag: _____

_____

Comments/Insights: _____

_____

DAY 2: THE HOUR APPROACHES

Tomorrow is the day. I hope that you had a good night's rest. If not, and you feel inclined to take a nap today, please do. Keep it under an hour, unless you got less than eight hours' sleep last night. If that's the case, nap as long as you would like, just as long as you'll still be able to go to sleep tonight. You know your body and sleep patterns better than I do. Follow your own wisdom for what will help you be in Optimal shape when it counts.

Eat a breakfast that is not out of the ordinary for you. If you do not normally eat breakfast, or have only coffee, now is not the time to change the habit. Continue doing whatever you do, but consider drinking fruit juice in addition to the water, as well as a piece of fruit or two. You may choose to have muffins, toast, bagels, cereal, or whatever. For right now, the important thing is to stick with your usual morning routine.

> *Find a way
> to lighten up.*

Before or after breakfast, I would ask that you engage in some type of light activity, preferably outdoors. Take a nice walk. It will maintain your energy and help you clear your mind of anything other than performing well. If you saw a good comedy yesterday, or something else that took your mind off the upcoming event without requiring much energy, I would recommend more of the same today.

If you were not able to do that, and at this point have lost your sense of humor, it is very important that you find a way to lighten up. This is not life and death. If you need to laugh, please do so. Rent a good video; check out HBO or the Comedy Channel. Your sense of humor will be a wonderful ally when you go into battle.

One thing that you may be able to do, as part of the Attunement process, is to make a site visit to the place where you'll be performing. Check out the locations where you'll warm up and perform. Finalize your Attentional Plan, reviewing where you'll put your Attention after you get there.

Then Center and imagine yourself performing just the way you would like to. Take your time. Once you are pleased with what you see, hear, and feel, take a walk around the perimeter of the room. Pause at different spots, look back to where you will be performing, and imagine yourself there, doing great and enjoying the process. Then get to a point as far away as possible from your starting place, while still being able to see it.

Center again, then look around and take it all in. Get a sense of control over everything you see. Then focus on where you will be standing or sitting. Imagine yourself there, starting out well, with your beautiful sound and image going out into the space. Again, notice how good you feel in this space. Embrace it.

Next, go back onstage or into the room in which you'll perform. Center, make the commitment again that you are going to Go For It, and then smile. From this point on, the mindset is: it will be fine. If there are any questions from now until you actually do walk off tomorrow, that is the answer: "It will be fine." This is the mantra I encourage you to repeat: "It will be fine." And it will.

For the rest of the day, take it easy. Practice the performance skill of biding your time well in the last twenty-four hours. Stay loose; preserve your vital energy. Simplify what you eat from now until you leave for your performance, and keep drinking plenty of water. For this evening's meal, have something fairly bland—something that will be easy to digest yet give you some energy tomorrow. Hang in there. You're almost there.

TRAINING LOG
DAY 2

Date: _____ Day of the Week: _____

Amount of Sleep Last Night: _____

Length of Nap(s) Yesterday: _____

Glasses of Water Yesterday: _____

Length of Exercise/Walk: _____

Effective Ways for Biding Your Time: _____

_____

Attunement: _____

_____

Attentional Plan: _____

_____

Comments/Insights: _____

_____

DAY 1: YOU HAVE ARRIVED

Today's the day. Are you ready for takeoff? You should feel like you are sitting on top of a rocket ship by now; so keep your seat belt securely fastened. It's going to get even more exciting in the next few hours.

Before you get to your performance site, put your guard up. Do not underestimate the upcoming situation. Get ready for a fight: a knock-down, drag-out fight. That is why you'll need your boundary. This is no longer going to be fun and games. This is now about more serious stuff. I hope you know you're ready.

> *Trust your talent and training and Let It Fly!*

Once you get to your performance site, it's important that you keep your mind on the process and the task at hand. All you need to do is to perform it the way you rehearsed: nothing special. There is no need for anything extra. Remember that you are striving for an Optimal Performance, not perfection. Go through your routine and get ready to do what you've been doing.

Keep your intention clear about your Mission. Center and use your energy to focus and accomplish what you've practiced and envisioned. Then you'll be able to walk out with your head high, proud for having done your best.

Keep three principles in mind. Number One is that what you think is what you get. If you think that you're going to have an Optimal

Performance, you probably will. If you think that you're going to mess up, I guarantee that you will. Remember, it will be fine.

Number Two: What you fear, you attract. Fear is a very powerful emotion: be careful today to focus only on what you courageously intend to do. Commit ahead of time to Go For It, and then follow your plan.

Number Three: We create our own reality with our thoughts and actions. Realize that you are the cause of everything that you experience and have in your life. Why not choose to create what you would like to experience?

Maintain the image, feeling, and sound of performing your best and accomplishing your Mission. Trust your talent and training and Let It Fly!

Enjoy the ride.

TRAINING LOG
DAY 1

Date: _____ Day of the Week: _____

Amount of Sleep Last Night: _____

Length of Nap(s) Yesterday: _____

Glasses of Water Yesterday: _____

Length of Exercise/Walk: _____

Here's the drill: perform at least two of your repertoire selections, plus three requests from your sponsor and guests. When you've finished, make some comments in your log. Mention what you did well and what you need to improve next time. Complete the evaluation and ask your sponsor and guests to complete them as well. Then enjoy the party.

FNAL PERFORMANCE

Date: _____ Time: _____ Location: _____

Part/Piece/ Excerpt	Rating	Strengths	Areas to Improve
_____	_____	_____	_____
_____	_____	_____	_____
_____	_____	_____	_____

Comments/Insights: _____

_____

_____

_____

Evaluator's Name: _____

Part/Piece/   Rating   Comments
Excerpt

_____   _____   _____

_____   _____   _____

_____   _____   _____

Evaluator's Name: _____

Part/Piece/   Rating   Comments
Excerpt

_____   _____   _____

_____   _____   _____

_____   _____   _____

Evaluator's Name: _____

Part/Piece/   Rating   Comments
Excerpt

_____   _____   _____

_____   _____   _____

_____   _____   _____

Comments/Insights: _____

_____

Take a break. If possible, take a few days off. You deserve it. If you'd like to do anything extra special today, please do. In the next week, treat yourself to a reward that will remind you of what you've accomplished. Also make sure to give your sponsor and guests some type of symbol of your appreciation. Whenever you're ready, take the Artist's Performance Survey again, based on today's performance. From that point on, you know what to do. All my very best to you.

Appendix 1

Dear Sponsor,

In naming you as sponsor, the owner of this book is demonstrating how much your relationship and support matters. Thanks in advance for all your help.

You will need to be available for three important performances: seven, fourteen, and twenty-one days from now. Please check the Countdown schedule on page 106. Of particular importance is your role at the end of next week.

You've likely been cheering your friend along for some time now. To help prepare him or her to deal with the inevitable difficulties of live performances, you'll be setting up an Adverse Mock Performance on Day 8 of the Countdown. If you are unable to do these things, let your friend know immediately.

Your friend has prepared three repertoire selections and will be expecting some sight-reading. You will set up the space to resemble a performance or audition, then arrange several "surprises," such as loud sounds, interruptions, or other challenges. The rest is fair game. Be creative, but keep it realistic.

To give you some ideas, here's what the New World Symphony Fellows did last year as part of their Adversity Training. They waited in an overheated green room for a half-hour without their instruments. Then they were called one at a time without knowing who would be next. After running up and down three flights of stairs, they had only thirty seconds to warm up.

They had to walk through a maze of chairs and equipment to get to their music stands. The stage was overcooled. They faced a screen that hid a panel of judges. These folks made a lot of noise during the performance (ringing cell phones, stapling papers, and scooting chairs). Ten seconds into their first requested excerpt, the performers were told to stop and begin again. During other selections, there were loud radio blasts, dropped cello boards, and flash cameras going off. Blowing fans sent music off the stands. After being asked rapid-fire to play piece after piece, they were left in silence for thirty seconds before being presented with an obscure piece to sight-read.

Every one of them nailed the mock audition. In fact, one of them left for a professional audition the next day and won. He gave credit to the Adversity Training for his success. Within the experience, he found what worked for him under the circumstances. This is what I hope your friend will take away as well.

Afterward, you will evaluate the performance and make some observations.

Please find a small gift or reward to serve as positive reinforcement for your friend's efforts and progress. You might like to arrange a party or small celebration.

Your friend and I greatly appreciate your wonderful assistance.

Sincerely,

Don Greene

Appendix 2

ARTIST'S PERFORMANCE SCORING

1. Draw a line through all the scores in Scenario 2 and Scenario 3 and change them as follows:

$$1 \rightarrow 5 \qquad 2 \rightarrow 4 \qquad 4 \rightarrow 2 \qquad 5 \rightarrow 1$$

2. Add your four numerical responses to determine your score in each category. For example, the Intrinsic Motivation category is comprised of your responses to questions 1, 4, 64, 89: (4), (4), (3), and (3) for a total of 14. Multiply your total by 5 for your score $(14 \times 5 = 70)$.

3. Circle that score (90) next to the Intrinsic Motivation category.

FACTOR 1: DETERMINATION

Intrinsic Motivation	*Commitment*	*Will to Succeed*
1) _____	2) _____	3) _____
4) _____	6) _____	63) _____
64) _____	65) _____	88) _____
89) _____	90) _____	91) _____
Subtotal _____	_____	_____
× 5		
Total _____	**Total** _____	**Total** _____

FACTOR 2: POISE

Optimal Activation	Rehearsal Activation	Performance Activation	Audition Activation
10) _____	19) _____	22) _____	24) _____
32) _____	20) _____	69) _____	25) _____
33) _____	21) _____	82) _____	70) _____
54) _____	55) _____	83) _____	87) _____
Total _____	Total _____	Total _____	Total _____

Performance under Pressure	Ability to Activate	Ability to Deactivate
5) _____	23) _____	34) _____
39) _____	68) _____	35) _____
53) _____	80) _____	57) _____
92) _____	81) _____	59) _____
Total _____	Total _____	Total _____

FACTOR 3: MENTAL OUTLOOK

Self-Confidence	Self-Talk	Expectancy
9) _____	46) _____	8) _____
12) _____	49) _____	30) _____
28) _____	67) _____	51) _____
40) _____	94) _____	76) _____
Total _____	Total _____	Total _____

FACTOR 4: EMOTIONAL APPROACH

Ability to Risk	Risking Defeat	Risking Success
29) _____	11) _____	7) _____
58) _____	26) _____	36) _____
84) _____	38) _____	74) _____
98) _____	56) _____	85) _____
Total _____	Total _____	Total _____

FACTOR 5: CONTROLLING ATTENTION

Object of Focus	*Focus Past Distractions*	*Mental Quiet*
18) _____	17) _____	43) _____
27) _____	42) _____	45) _____
37) _____	60) _____	96) _____
86) _____	93) _____	97) _____
Total _____	**Total** _____	**Total** _____

FACTOR 6: CONCENTRATION

Intensity of Focus	*Presence of Focus*	*Duration of Focus*
14) _____	15) _____	16) _____
41) _____	71) _____	44) _____
62) _____	73) _____	72) _____
75) _____	95) _____	100) _____
Total _____	**Total** _____	**Total** _____

FACTOR 7: RESILIENCE

Ability to Fight	*Ease Under Pressure*	*Ability to Recover*
13) _____	47) _____	48) _____
31) _____	50) _____	66) _____
52) _____	61) _____	77) _____
79) _____	99) _____	78) _____
Total _____	**Total** _____	**Total** _____

Recommended Reading

The Book of Positive Quotations, compiled and edited by John Cook, Fairview Press, Minneapolis, MN, 1993.

Feel the Fear and Do It Anyway, Susan Jeffers, Ph.D., Ballantine Books, New York, 1987.

Zen in the Art of Archery, Eugen Herrigel, Random House, New York, 1981.

Think, Dr. Robert Anthony, The Berkeley Publishing Group, New York, 1983.

Power Sleep: The Revolutionary Program That Prepares Your Mind for Peak Performance, Dr. James B. Maas, Villard Books, New York, 1998.

The New Toughness Training for Sports, James E. Loehr, Penguin Books, New York, 1994.

Illusions: The Adventures of a Reluctant Messiah, Richard Bach, Dell Publishing, New York, 1977.

Psycho-Cybernetics, Maxwell Maltz, Prentice-Hall, Englewood Cliffs, NJ, 1960.

ML 3830 .G74 2002
Greene, Don.
Performance success

DATE DUE
